Mary Mackie was born in Lincoln during the Second World War. After leaving school she worked as an accounts clerk before she met and married her husband Chris, who was in the RAF. They spent some years in Berlin and West Germany and it was there that she began her career as a writer. She has had 65 books published, mostly fiction. Her second book about life in a National Trust house, *Dry Rot and Daffodils*, is also published by Orion. Her husband was the Administrator of Felbrigg Hall in Norfolk until 1990 and they still live in East Anglia.

## By Mary Mackie

# Cobwebs and Cream Teas

*A year in the life of a National Trust house*

## MARY MACKIE

ORION

For all staff and friends of Felbrigg Hall

And in memory of a very dear father,
CHARLES WILLIAM EDWARD WHITLAM

An Orion paperback

First published in Great Britain in 1990
by Victor Gollancz Ltd
This paperback edition published in 1995
by Victor Gollancz

Reissued in 2001
by Orion Books Ltd,
Orion House, 5 Upper St Martin's Lane,
London WC2H 9EA

Third Impression 2002

A CIP catalogue record for this book is available
from the British Library.

ISBN 0 75283 410 X

Printed and bound in Great Britain by
The Guernsey Press Co. Ltd, Guernsey, C.I.

# Contents

# 1

## Novices in Norfolk

Remembering our first encounter with Felbrigg Hall, I'm irresistibly reminded of all the horror movies I've ever seen.

It was October. All morning, as my husband and I drove from Lincolnshire into Norfolk, rain clouds had been gathering. Now the storm was about to break. The sky darkened into swirling, livid steel as we map-read our way along a final three miles of country lanes and came at last to wrought-iron gates where a sign read 'Felbrigg Hall'.

Beyond twin grey lodges, the drive wound away into gloom, through a tunnel of oak trees whose trunks were lost in an impenetrable tangle of rhododendron bushes. Our headlights cut a pale swathe through the weird storm-light. The wind hurled fistfuls of leaves to scatter across the windscreen. The drive seemed to run on for ever, round a bend, over a hill. At last we glimpsed a building—a church, pale and grey beneath the scudding sky, standing forsaken behind a freshly ploughed field.

And then suddenly, ahead of us, through shadows cast by the approaching storm, the ancient house appeared, gaunt and forbidding in a grandeur of castellated turrets and Jacobean bays. In that moment the first rain swept down, throwing curtains of obscurity across the view. Was it an omen? Dare we approach the forbidding mansion? What fate awaited us there . . . ?

We had come to Norfolk in response to an advertisement for the post of Houseman with the National Trust at Felbrigg Hall. The opportunity came at a good time for us—my husband, Chris, had wearied of being tied to an office desk as an internal auditor in big business and was seeking a new challenge while he was still young enough to take it; our two sons were grown and flown—the elder one at university, the younger just starting to train as a nurse (in Norwich, fortuitously)—and my own work, as a freelance writer, can be carried on anywhere. Working for the National Trust would provide an escape from the rat race, a change to a quieter, less stressful lifestyle for both of us.

At least—that was what we thought at the time. We could hardly believe our luck when Chris was short-listed and we were both summoned to an interview.

The job description called for a man who could adapt himself to any situation concerning meeting the public, taking cash and doing basic administration, plus generally maintaining and caring for a great country house under the guidance of the administrator. All of these things Chris could do without any problem; he is a great handyman and DIY enthusiast, besides being a professional accountant with the enviable ability to think on his feet in any situation. I knew he was the perfect man for the job.

Whether the interview panel felt the same it was difficult to tell. They spent some time chatting about my own career, the books I had published and so forth, and then astounded me by suggesting that I might like to run the National Trust shop at Felbrigg—a prospect so unexpected that I could only goggle in disbelief and stammer my total lack of suitability, or inclination. As we drove home to Lincolnshire that evening I had a dreadful feeling that I might have spoiled Chris's chances.

However, a few days later we learned that he had been appointed. In a little over a month, we had to pack up our belongings and move to Norfolk.


It was a bleak, cold Sunday in November when we arrived, along with our eighteen-year-old younger son, Kevin, to camp out in our new home, anticipating the arrival of our furniture next day. The first-floor flat, in a rear wing of the Hall, had been newly modernised, with sitting room, bathroom, kitchen and two bed-

Suddenly, ahead of us, the ancient house
appeared, gaunt and forbidding . . .

rooms all set to one side of a long corridor. Though small after
the four-bedroom house we had left behind, the flat was very
pleasant and convenient.

The main Hall had closed for the season at the end of October,
but the shop would be open until Christmas and the tea-room
was serving its usual hot soup, tea and scones. We were plunged
straight into involvement: within an hour of our arrival, an
urgent call up the stairs summoned us to the aid of the tea-room
ladies, who had run out of milk. Chris had to go and find the
nearest Sunday-opening store, which was about five miles away.

The following day the furniture van arrived on time, but
the men were dismayed to discover they could not get their
pantechnicon near our door. They had to carry everything
through a wrought-iron gateway, fifty yards across a grass courtyard, through a door and along an L-shaped lobby, down three
steps, through another door and into a tiny hall where they were
confronted by two flights of stairs boasting a very awkward
angle. At the top, in the flat proper, they faced the added rigours

of a long corridor with rooms off and more steps, seven up, six down, where our central two rooms lay over the high-ceilinged kitchen of the Hall. Phew! I learned some colourful language that day, and lost count of how many pots of tea I brewed in an effort to placate the removal men.

In the middle of all this, Eve, the administrator's wife, fell over their dog and broke her ankle. Chris had to take her to Casualty in Cromer hospital; her husband Robert was, of course, the only one competent to take care of the Hall, so he had to remain on duty. Meanwhile, I was left to supervise the moving-in.

That first chaotic day provided a good foretaste of what life could be like at Felbrigg!

Among other tasks during our first few weeks, Chris and I spent hours out in the Rose Garden measuring and selling Christmas trees. It was very cold, but lovely with frost across the park, a distant mist, and the sun sinking red behind the woods in the afternoon. We met some delightful people, among them a couple who offered to bring us a box of apples from the local Pick-Your-Own orchards—and did so. It was all so very different from our former lives that we kept wanting to pinch ourselves to believe we were really there.

Meanwhile, in our flat, as we slowly settled in and organised our belongings, there were problems to iron out. Although plumbing for a washing machine had been installed in the spacious kitchen/diner, the worktop was too low to allow the machine under it. Workmen soon came to put that right. Then, trying to lay our carpets, we discovered that several old doors were set too low for them to open over carpet. A carpenter came to trim the necessary half inch or so, loosening the old hinges and removing the doors before this could be accomplished.

On one of the doors a four-inch-deep piece of wood had been added to the bottom at some time, presumably because of rotting; this extra piece had been nailed on, as the carpenter now discovered, with giant hand-made nails nearly six inches long. We still have one of these; it makes a fascinating conversation piece.

Was it fashioned by one of the workers on the estate, many years ago?

Soon after we arrived, Eve warned me of the dangers of becoming too deeply involved as an unpaid extra pair of hands. She herself had a full-time career which kept her away from the Hall during the week, but she foresaw that I might have difficulties; I worked from home and would be on the spot, on call all the time.

I suppose I was too new to it all, too euphoric to take her advice seriously; I thought she must be exaggerating. But I ought to have paid more attention, especially when I had a foretaste of what might come. . . .

At the time, the Hall phone was connected to only two places —the office and an extension in the administrator's flat. There was also a very loud bell which rang in a downstairs corridor in case the only person available to answer it was far away in the depths of the house.

Only a couple of weeks after we moved in, I sat with Eve one day, drinking coffee and keeping her company while she was incapacitated with her broken ankle. The phone kept ringing every few minutes and, since both our husbands were otherwise engaged in duties about the Hall, I was acting telephonist to save my hostess from constantly leaping up with her leg in plaster.

It was just before Christmas and we were inundated with calls about the stock in the shop:

"Have you got the blue tablecloths?" someone would ask, or, "Are there any puddings left?" or table mats of certain design, or Christmas trees. . . . The only way to answer such queries was to take the caller's number, go down to the shop and ascertain the facts, then return and phone back the potential customer with the answer.

This had been going on for days. No wonder Eve was weary.

Being the 'new girl', fresh to the task and somewhat ingenuous, I rushed to and from the shop all afternoon, up and down eighteen stairs and along 100 yards of stone corridor each time. I was eager to do my bit and impress our customers with my efficiency—though I must admit that after a dozen or so such calls my enthusiasm was beginning to wane.

"You'll learn," warned Eve, wiser than I in the ways of the Trust; then she remarked in wonder, "Do you realise you actually *smile* when you answer the wretched phone?"

This narrative is based mainly on what happened during our first year at Felbrigg Hall; in that way, it's a personal record. But having met and talked with staff (and spouses) from other properties across the country, I know that our experience typifies, in general, what goes on inside most National Trust houses.

One thing I can say for the life—it's never boring. Hard work, with long hours—yes, always. Often frustrating, sometimes delightful, interspersed with scenes of high drama, touches of broad farce and moments of magic. But tedious? Never! There's really only one way to understand it, and that's to live it, day by day.

Let me offer you the chance of doing just that, here in these pages. Come and spend a year with us—a year behind the scenes with the National Trust.

## 2

# Winter—The 'Closed' Season

### A Portrait of Felbrigg

Thanks to a throw-away line in a Noël Coward play, a calumny exists that Norfolk is flat. It is not. The area around Felbrigg, in the north of the county, is a landscape of hills and hollows, rolling fields and shady woods, dotted with pretty, hidden villages. One of the things we love is the unspoilt beauty of the countryside—the vistas that change as one drives the narrow lanes, and especially the many woods and copses which in autumn can be a glory. Nearby Roman Camp is reputed to lie on the highest point in the county, while Sheringham, Cromer and resorts to the east boast magnificent cliffs sheltering sandy or pebbled beaches.

This, then, is the setting in which Felbrigg Hall is placed, with its back to the north, sheltered from the coldest winds by a shawl of lovingly planted woodland.

The most ancient part of the house is a dank medieval under-croft, now part of the cellars, probably dating from the fourteenth century. It is thick with shadows, crawling with the occasional toad and lizard; in wet weather rain drips through from the courtyard above. Intriguingly, nothing is known of the manor house which once stood over this cellar. It belonged to the Norman lords de Felbrigg, one of whom, Sir Simon, was standard-bearer to Richard II. Signs of early foundations were found when drains were excavated a few years ago, but the evidence was too scanty to provide many clues.

Above ground, the oldest part of today's Hall, built by Sir

John Wyndham and his son Thomas Windham, is Jacobean; three large south-facing bays, extending through two floors but only one room deep, comprised the manor which was completed about 1624. Further wings, the latest being the castellated Regency stable yard, were added as the centuries progressed. The result is a pleasing sprawl of red brick, stone quoins and faded stucco topped by elegant chimneys. From the parapets gaze stone lions, unicorns and gryphons, freckled with lichen, keeping watch over the quiet courtyards below.

A bird's-eye view of Felbrigg Hall roughly resembles an E with the lower section forming a square courtyard and with a stable yard added on below; the back of the E is the south front of the house. The Orangery is the separate building at the top, beyond the west wing. It is an impressive sprawl of buildings. The main Hall as it stands today—not counting stables, outhouses or the tenanted apartments around the rear courtyard—consists of about fifty rooms, though not all of these are open to visitors. The total includes store rooms, offices, and the two private flats, plus the expansive attics and cellars. The attics too are used as store rooms, though the cellars for the most part remain empty.

Although we are a mile from the nearest public road, and three miles from the small coastal resort of Cromer, we are not lonely; around the rear courtyard lives a small community of tenants and staff, about twelve people in all. There are also working farms on the estate, run by tenant farmers, and the two gate lodges are occupied, one by tenants, the other used by the head gardener and his family.

The house sits serene in the middle of parkland dotted with trees, with views over fields where young calves are being born from spring to summer. Around it stretch five hundred acres of lovely woods, and we have a lake where fishing is allowed from June to September. In all, the estate covers about seventeen hundred acres. It is supervised from regional office by our land agent and our head forester. Our own head woodsman lives at the Hall with his wife; he and his assistants have the day-to-day responsibility for all the woods on the estate.

The church with its curious grey box pews stands about a

The hall and courtyards

quarter of a mile away, a grey nave and tower stranded now in
the middle of pastureland. Its brasses are among the finest in the
country; they include a sumptuous memorial commemorating
Sir Simon de Felbrigg and his wife. He it was who rebuilt the
church in the early fifteenth century. It is dedicated to St Margaret
of Antioch. In 1924, when Wyndham Cremer Cremer inherited
the estate, the church was almost derelict, but he and his wife
undertook its restoration and in 1968 their son, R. W. Ketton-
Cremer, donated the statue of St Margaret and the dragon, which
stands above the south porch. It looks like stone but is in fact
made of fibre-glass.

The church is still used for services, when we hear its bell
tolling out across the park to summon the faithful.

What happened to the village which once surrounded the
church is a matter for speculation. Today's Felbrigg village lies

half a mile away. Did it move because of the Black Death, or was it an eyesore to some arrogant squire, who had it removed? No one knows for sure; it's one of Felbrigg's many enigmas.

When the de Felbrigg family died out in 1461, the estates came into the care of the Wyndham (later Windham) family, who held them for four hundred years. The early Windhams seem to have been turbulent squires, constantly at odds with their neighbours, especially the Pastons. Through varying fortunes and vicissitudes, succeeding generations continued at Felbrigg until 1863, when bankruptcy forced the selling of the estate. But, via a rather convoluted route, Wyndham descendants came back into their Felbrigg heritage two generations later.

Felbrigg was bequeathed to the National Trust in 1969 by its last owner, the bachelor writer and historian Mr Robert Wyndham Ketton-Cremer, 'the Squire', who is fondly remembered by local people. His book, *Felbrigg—the Story of a House*, is a fascinating read, full of information about the Hall and the families who lived there.

Anyone walking in Felbrigg park in the chill, quiet days of the early year may be forgiven for assuming the place is hibernating. A frost lies white on pasture churned to mud and a red sun hangs in a bleak sky. Trees lift bare branches, like gaunt ghosts clad in shreds of mist, and through that mist the house is a dark shape backed by a cloak of sombre woods. It appears to be sleeping, locked and blinded behind pale shutters.

But come closer and you may see that here and there a faint light glimmers. Piles of sand and bricks, with a concrete mixer and maybe a skip for rubbish, blemish the elegant environs; cars and commercial vans are crammed into the stable yard. And if you draw near enough you may hear the winter chorus of hammers, drills and saws, vacuum cleaners and floor scrubbers; clatterings, bangings, tearings of wood, rending of lath and plaster. . . .

Inside the house, winter days can be even more hectic than during the height of the season.

## Winter Routines

During the first full week of the New Year, the work of the Hall resumes in earnest.

The administrator will generally be found in the office, finalising plans for concerts and other events, arranging for workmen to see to repairs and maintenance, co-ordinating visits from the management team at regional office, making phone calls, writing letters. . . . One of his most complicated and time-consuming tasks at this time of year is the organising of the room wardens' roster for the coming season. But as in every other organisation, a great deal of routine office work is also necessary to keep a National Trust property functioning. Most of it is done by the administrator.

Meanwhile the houseman will be occupied with more practical tasks, especially supervising the winter cleaning and conservation which move back into top gear with the return of the cleaners from their Christmas break. And in between the major tasks there are a hundred and one smaller things to do. The houseman must be a handyman able to cope with any job that might crop up in a huge old house—electrical emergencies, broken windows, blocked drains, cleaning, painting, guarding against woodworm and other pests . . . the list is endless.

Winter too is the time when any major renovations take place. In our first year Felbrigg was to play host to two or three teams of workmen contracted from a local building firm. Supervising them and liaising with their foremen kept the house staff busy. Everything—the cleaning schedule and the repair works—had to be co-ordinated to a conclusion by the end of March, when we were due to open again to the public.

We soon got into the rhythm of the winter routine. Every weekday, it was Chris's job to open up the house, unfasten shutters to let light in and put on heaters to alleviate the bone-deep chill before workmen and cleaners arrived. Around eight o'clock, the first of the workmen would be ringing the bell at the rear entrance, waiting for Chris to unlock the 'Green Door' and let them in.

Not many minutes later, the Hall would reverberate with hammering, sawing, clattering, possibly whistling—sounds to accompany whatever job was in progress—plus the raising of much dust, the bringing down of old ceilings in forgotten, seldom-seen areas, and strange damp, fusty odours that filled the air as the old building was disturbed. When the men came across rot, or fraying wires, or some other unexpected complication, they stopped work and summoned Chris to advise them. He in turn might consult Robert, the administrator, and if further skilled opinion was needed there were always Trust specialists to be called upon.

At the time, our stalwart team of cleaners comprised four local ladies (the number has since been depleted to three). During the winter they work from 9 a.m. to 12, Monday to Friday, a mere fifteen hours a week, during which they accomplish the spring-cleaning of the entire house and most of the contents, work that once demanded a full complement of housemaids.

An extra task that first January was to clear the Morning Room and prepare it for stripping by experts. Dry rot had been discovered; the room had to be completely empty before workmen could begin to tackle the problem.

Since none of the ladies is a Brunhilde, Chris helped them to move some of the furniture. Weightier and trickier items, such as pictures—especially the enormous Morning Room portraits —had to be handled with particular care and, to save time for the cleaners, were often taken down and put away from harm during the afternoons and evenings. The administrator, plus myself, any visiting (adult) offspring and friends, and/or our ever-obliging gardeners were variously called in to help with this sort of job. Some pictures are very high up, and very heavy; they required the assistance of scaffolding in order that they might be moved safely, without damage to canvas or delicate frames. Erecting the scaffolding was another time-consuming job, as was taking it down again. Finally, when the walls were clear and the furniture stored elsewhere, the carpet was rolled up—pile side out, in order not to stretch it. Achieving this with a very large, very heavy, valuable old carpet was another major operation requiring the help of all available hands.

With the Morning Room now empty, the dry rot specialists moved in to strip the floor-to-ceiling oak panelling from the walls and take up floorboards, reducing the room to its basic structure in order to deal with the fungus. The resulting mess and chaos can be imagined.

One day Chris was sweeping up the worst of the grit when one of the men called him—look, see that? Know what it is?

Not only was the room riddled with dry rot, the panelling was infested with death-watch beetle. Urgent calls to regional office reported this new problem.

## The Secret Stair

When news of the Morning Room seemed all depression, among the doom and gloom Felbrigg had a surprise in store—it was about to reveal the first of the secrets with which it has continued to delight us over the years.

When the workmen, chasing the extent of the dry rot, stripped back some of the floorboards, they came across a rubble-filled, wedge-shaped depression that looked like the first step of a flight of stairs. Curious, they reported this discovery and were asked to clear some of the rubble. They uncovered three steps before they were forced to stop because the way was solidly blocked.

Evidently there was once a stairway connecting this area—which was originally the kitchen and buttery—with the cellar below. The stair was at some time done away with; there is nothing left of it in the cellar. But if you look very closely, with the aid of a torch in the dark that pervades down there, you can discern the line arc-ing across the barrel roof, where the gap was plastered over to blend with the rest. As far as we could discover, no one had suspected that this stair had ever existed.

The find fascinated us all; it gave us another small insight into the history of the house. Before the three steps were, of necessity, refilled with rubble and covered up, not to be seen again for who knows how many years, Chris took some photographs of them. It was to be the beginning of another sideline for him—recording evidence of Felbrigg's intimate secrets, for his own interest and for posterity.

Discovering the secret stair

Having cleared the Morning Room, the cleaners were able to continue their regular winter routine. They had to work swiftly that year; before Christmas they had been manning the tea-room, so the conservation work was well behind schedule. The main rooms had been draped in dust sheets and the porcelain and smaller items stored together under acid-free paper, but that was all. The entire house was supposed to be spring-cleaned before the end of March. Compromises would have to be made.

They began at the top of the building, with the job that is their least favourite—sweeping and dusting half-lit corridors and rooms full of accumulated bric-à-brac, in the attics.

A fire-alarm engineer was also in the Hall checking and renovating the complicated fire-alarm system; at various times he needed access to all parts of the house, including the attics and the private flats. Chris kept track of his progress, so that locked doors didn't cause him delays.

Work in one of the corridors and the shop continued from before Christmas, caused by trouble with the drains, which seemed to have its source somewhere under the flagstones of the Red Corridor, so-called because it is painted a deep red; the flagstones were up, the water channels exposed. Workmen clumped in and out bringing in mud, raising dust and dirt which they tramped into the floors—another job for the houseman.

Elsewhere, painters were putting finishing touches to redecoration. And from time to time all kinds of maintenance men turned up to see to the servicing of equipment—cookers, fridges, hand-dryers in the cloakrooms and so forth: a score of different appliances had to be serviced before the season started.

In any house, all this activity would be frustrating. In a large National Trust property the distances involved, plus the vital matter of security, add their own problems. Teams of workmen seem to have different lunch hours, and different knocking-off times. All of them need to be let in, or out. The houseman sometimes feels as though he has spent most of his day rushing to answer the door, the bell constantly interrupting whatever else he may be trying to do.

A terrific thunderstorm broke over us, shaking the ancient walls, rattling loose Jacobean leaded windows, puddling water in contrary places and, as a special favour, cutting the power supply to every part of the Hall. Inside the house, robbed of light, everyone peered through grey gloaming, doing whatever could be done without power: most of the workmen decided to take a mid-morning break and went to sit in their vans in the stable yard, where the smokers among them could indulge their habit, not being allowed to smoke inside the house; the cleaners were about to have their coffee in the butler's pantry—a room without windows; in sudden blackness their kettle stopped singing. When Chris took a torch to their aid, they groped their way back to the attics where small windows gave them just enough light to continue removing a year's accumulation of cobwebs, bat droppings and fallen plaster.

Meanwhile Robert had contacted the electricity board, whose engineers arrived and set out to locate the junction box, which is attached to a telegraph pole in the woods. Fifteen minutes later, they were back. Where, exactly, was the junction box, please? Chris donned a waterproof and set out to lead them to the spot.

Have you ever tried to locate one particular telegraph pole in a wood full of straight-trunked sycamore, in bad light and with rain pouring down? Eventually, the intrepid explorers attained their goal and restored light to our darkness. Work continued again.

During the storm, ingenious rain found several new avenues into the house; it dripped into the corridor where the men had flagstones up, so now another hazard was added for the unwary —buckets to collect the drips! Chris spent many happy hours tracing and plugging all the leaks.

## The Library

The cleaners moved on to the Library. This spacious room was altered by one of Felbrigg's scholar squires to accommodate his collection. He had a window blocked up, which leaves the room rather dark, but it is lined on all four walls with thousands of leather-bound books. All of them have been read and re-read by the families who owned them, and they are still available to scholars. Some date back to the early years of printing; some are almost too heavy to carry; some are large and unwieldy in shape; many are of great value, and all are precious as part of Felbrigg's contents. We even have some books which belonged to Samuel Johnson, annotated in his hand and bequeathed to his great friend William Windham III, a squire of Felbrigg who was also Secretary-at-War under Pitt in the closing years of the eighteenth century.

Every volume is checked at least once a year, shelves cleaned, walls and ceiling brushed and furniture cared for. When cleaning books the ladies work in a team, wearing white cotton gloves to prevent oil from their skin damaging pages and leather bindings. One lady will be on a library ladder taking down the volumes very carefully, one at a time, handing each book to one of her colleagues who dusts the top of the book and the fly leaves with the softest possible shaving brush before looking through the pages for signs of damage through damp, fungus, worm, or . . .

"Beetle!" The discovery sent consternation through the ladies and they summoned Chris. Inside one of the books, a death-watch beetle larva, hatching near the book's spine, had chewed a tunnel that widened as the insect grew, moving through the book towards the fore-edge, where the fully-fledged adult had been only a millimetre away from breaking through and flying off to lay its own damaging offspring elsewhere in the library. Chris still has the beetle, enshrined in a plastic bag.

The operation of cleaning all the books may take anything from five weeks to two months.

We were expecting a visit from the head housekeeper, who is based at National Trust headquarters in London. She visits all of the Trust's mansions on a regular basis, to oversee the cleaning work, give advice on preferred techniques and help with any special problems which may have arisen. The historic buildings representative (HBR) for the region was to accompany her on this occasion.

The head housekeeper and the HBR were to be at Felbrigg for a whole day, so naturally they required entertaining to lunch. Because the administrator's wife had a job which kept her away from the Hall during the week, the houseman's wife was elected hostess for the occasion. Though I was nervous at the prospect of entertaining Trust VIPs they assured me they would be happy with soup and a roll so that's more or less what I gave them. Robert, our administrator, joined us, too, and the occasion passed very pleasantly, amid interesting and informative conversation.

It was becoming evident that with my husband working for the National Trust it was impossible for me to remain uninvolved.


Cleaners and workmen don't usually come in on Saturday and Sunday during the winter, so from Christmas to March administrator and houseman can usually take alternate weekends off. For the person left on duty, routine work goes on—the mail must be dealt with, the phone answered, callers seen to and trespassers confronted.

Anticipating his retirement, Robert had bought a country cottage to which he and Eve repaired for two days every fortnight, when he had a well-earned respite from ringing phones and jangling door bells. Our own free days we spent shopping, walking the woods or visiting places of interest (not easy on winter weekends in north Norfolk!).

Quite frequently, we found ourselves doing things for the Trust.

There was always something needed—photocopying, new plugs, locks, torch batteries, replacement tools . . . the list altered with every week. Some specialist items could be found only in Norwich and since there was no time for Chris to make a trip to the city during the working week these things had to be sought out and purchased on days off. Many times we spent our Saturday walking miles trying to locate exotica such as the right weight of chain to support a chandelier, or the scarce, old-fashioned, gold silk-covered lamp flex which would be more in keeping with the ambience of the house than the modern plastic kind. Still, it was more interesting than ordinary shopping and did give us something to occupy an often cold, wet, rather aimless day.

## The Attics

Living so close to his work, Chris finds it hard to shut the door and forget it even when he is officially off-duty. Besides, as he still maintains with irrefutable logic, some jobs are easier when the house is not full of people requiring his attention. The list of 'Urgent jobs to be done' was especially lengthy in our first year, when a great deal of extra sorting out was necessary in preparation for alterations that were to be made.

In particular, little had been done to tidy up certain obscure, seldom-seen areas of the house, which remained much as they had been left by Mr Ketton-Cremer. Earlier efforts had concentrated on the main rooms, but now time had to be found to attend to these neglected places. So, for Chris that first winter, evenings and weekends were often as work-intensive as normal working hours.

To begin with he reorganised the attics and transported items from other parts of the house for storage, to clear space that was going to be needed for other purposes. Robert lent a hand when his own duties allowed, but Chris often chose to work when we were alone in the house, so I helped him. I volunteered mainly because I was afraid he would exhaust himself, and it did mean seeing something of him on occasion. Besides which, I was intrigued by the old house and fascinated to discover what it contained in its secret, cobwebby corners and behind time-stiffened cupboard doors.

Among smaller treasures, we discovered a helmet belonging to an officer of the militia, still in its box, and two chocolate boxes, in the shape of a harp and violin, complete with strings. Who bought them, we wondered, and to whom were they given? My imagination leapt at the hints of long-ago romance pushed to the back of an old cupboard, lying forgotten amid the dust and cobwebs.

We also came across the cook's book of recipes, collected from all kinds of sources, some in the shape of yellowed cuttings from newspapers or magazines, some written out in her own hand—a treasure to be edited for publication one day, maybe.

Often we worked all day and into the evening, lugging furniture, oddments, books—the sorts of things that get pushed into every-body's attic—up the back stairs (six flights of them), and then along dark corridors and into dusty, ill-lit attic rooms that were slowly being transformed from utter chaos into specific places for specific things. We sorted and transported and shifted, until we had established a room full of beds, another for pictures, a place for chairs, for wardrobes and chests, a store for fabrics. . . . The basic job of removal took weeks and it was months before the attics were finally sorted to Chris's satisfaction.

The attic rooms (which are not normally open to the public) were once used as bedrooms by the children of the family, along with sundry nurses, nannies and governesses. A bell still hangs in one attic from where a servant could, presumably, have been summoned. The old wallpaper with its attractive patterns, torn and faded now, can still be seen in most of the rooms.

In the 1860s, when the Ketton family lived at Felbrigg, Mrs Ketton wrote a diary which still exists. She recorded how her five daughters slept in the attic bedrooms, and told how they would gather of an evening in what they called the 'balcony hotel'—the only bedroom with a fireplace—to get warm by the fire before four of them made a dash to the chill of their own rooms.

However, if ghosts linger Chris and I have never sensed them, even in the gloom of a winter twilight. A pity. Those girls sound as if they might have been great fun to meet.

## It Never Rains . . .

Towards the end of January, thick snow fell, whitening the park and the woods, enough to cut us off for a few hours before one of the men, using an estate tractor, ploughed a way through to the road.

Snow at Felbrigg was a wondrous sight, a white carpet laid across park and fields, dazzling in sunlight and striped with long shadow. In the garden the trees were outlined in a thick white coat which lay along the branches and made blue-shadowed mounds out of rhododendron bushes. We enjoyed being the first to leave imprints in the crisp covering—apart from birds and small animals, including a fox whose tracks we traced until they vanished in undergrowth.

Somehow the postman and the milkman managed to reach us, and soon all the workmen were back applying themselves to their various jobs. But the snow stayed beautiful until it melted; it didn't turn ugly, salted and gritty, as had been our experience in towns, with traffic and people trampling it to wet and dirty slush.


On the day when the temperature rose above freezing point, we were expecting a television crew to do an interview and some filming. Anticipating a busy day ahead, Chris was up early, which turned out to be fortunate; as he opened the house ready for the cleaners he saw water seeping through the ceiling of an upper corridor. It was dripping on to a valuable and very heavy antique chest, which he moved at once and dried with a cloth; later the water-marks would need treating with linseed oil. Investigating further, he discovered that snow had blocked the gullies on the roof, so that melting ice couldn't escape. Water was building up, seeping under the slates, over the leads, flowing into the attics in numerous places in drips and little rivulets. If the leaks found their way into the rooms below, priceless objects were in danger of permanent damage.

Needing instant help, Chris roused me from my warm bed and for a while we ran up and down the six flights of back stairs finding and placing receptacles to catch the inflow—buckets, bowls, jugs, whatever we could muster. In between whiles, the door bell kept summoning Chris as workmen arrived, and at 9 o'clock when the cleaners reported for work and learned of the problem they joined us in our efforts to halt the flow. Soon the attics were littered with all manner of containers playing discordant plink-plonk-plunk variations on a theme of melting snow.

The only real solution to the problem was of course to clear the blockage on the roof and redirect the water at source. As soon as all the major leaks had been tapped, Chris got out the wooden shovels (metal would damage the lead), climbed through an attic door on to the leads, and started to shift the icy slush from the gullies. He hadn't had time even for a cup of coffee, let alone breakfast, but hardly had he started to clear the snow when the local television team arrived. In all the excitement we had forgotten they were due.

The television crew's brief was to film a short documentary piece for transmission on a local news programme. They wanted to interview the administrator, but Robert demurred—he confided later that nerves made him inarticulate in front of a camera —and asked Chris to do it. Chris had been working with the Trust for just two months and felt inadequate to the task, but fortunately he had had previous experience in dealing with the media. He just answered the questions and hoped he was saying the right things, all the time praying that the microphone wouldn't pick up the rumblings in his empty stomach.

Every half hour or so, he had to break off to make another foray up and down, to and from the attics, emptying the containers and going out on to the roof to clear more slush from gullies.

Intrigued by these activities, the film crew followed him and stood in the doorway under the eaves, taking shots of him outside on the roof. The rest of the interview they conducted amid the Victorian grandeur of the Great Hall, sitting on pink brocade sofas draped in dust sheets, with Chris in anorak and wellington boots—though as he pointed out his boots were spotless: they had been thoroughly cleaned in melting snow.

The interview, and other filming to illustrate it, took most of the day, though on screen it ran to no more than five minutes. It was to be only the first of many television appearances for Chris—handling the media is another skill required of the staff of a National Trust house.

## Diary of a Winter Day

Some days can be particularly fraught. One that my diary noted with chagrin occurred in February.

It was a day of freezing fog, the park fading behind banks of mist and icicles gathering among the trees. Robert was away for a couple of days, obliged to attend a distant funeral, so Chris was in sole charge and I was on standby to attend to phone calls in his absence.

The day started especially early, one of the painters having warned us he would be coming in at 7.30 a.m. in order to clock off before dark. This meant that Chris was up and about before 7 to ensure that the relevant parts of the house were open and unchilled before the painter arrived.

He consoled himself that at least he didn't have far to go to work, though he did have to get dressed up in two sweaters, warm trousers, scarf, anorak and even a hat when working in the Hall. Not for nothing is Felbrigg reputed to be the coldest house in Norfolk! But, as it happens, though unpleasant for humans, the cold, dry conditions are better for the preservation of books and furniture; it's heat, light and damp that do the worst damage.

From 8.30, another painter and a carpenter were at work in the private apartments, fixing and painting an extra door between our sitting room and the administrator's spare bedroom, necessary for privacy. We were getting to know some of these workmen quite well. They were all employed by a local building firm which does many different jobs for the Trust, so we saw the same men again and again as fresh maintenance problems cropped up.

At 8.50, one of the cleaners called in sick—one of those things that happen now and then. The other three ladies arrived at 9 o'clock, as usual, to continue working in the Library.

Chris's main preoccupation was currently the high-level cleaning in the bedrooms, dusting ceilings and cornices and removing cobwebs from picture frames. As ever, the work was constantly interrupted by other duties, but he was often glad of an excuse to come down from his step-ladder and seek warmth and company.

When the postman arrived, in the administrator's absence there was the morning mail to be dealt with. Anything urgent had to be answered at once—without benefit of clerical help except that provided by me and my typewriter. (Felbrigg doesn't boast any secretarial assistance, except for a clerk who comes in to help the administrator for three hours [sic] every week.) All morning the phone rang with various enquiries and messages, most of which I dealt with.

A stills photographer from the local television station arrived, as planned, at 10 o'clock to take pictures to correlate with the previous filming; naturally he could not be let loose in the Hall on his own, so Chris escorted him while he completed his assignment.

Elsewhere, the workmen who were continuing their repairs in the Red Corridor and shop area damaged an electrical cable hidden in the wall; they reported the accident to Chris, who had to make an urgent call to an electrician to fix it.

Late morning, one of the cleaners dropped the lid of a porcelain soap dish; she was distraught, in tears. Chris calmed her down and reassured her—he knew how careful she was; accidents, though rare, are all part of the job. But, since the damage could be repaired only by an expert, it was his duty to put in an immediate report and explain how the accident happened.

The cleaners left at 12 but Chris worked on his ceilings for another hour, finally coming up to our flat for lunch at 1.10 p.m., after locking up behind the last workman.

At 1.15, just as we sat down for lunch, the phone rang yet again: someone wanted to know if we were open to visitors and if not, why not. The man was almost abusive when told he couldn't bring his friends to visit the Hall during the winter.

Chris had just sat down again to his meal when the door bell rang; answering it involved a long trek out of the flat, down all those stairs, through the tea-room, and along two corridors to the tradesman's entrance. The caller was someone from regional office who, since he happened to be passing, had kindly taken the opportunity to deliver a batch of new garden guides, several heavy boxes which would later need storing out of the way up yet more stairs. The weary Chris returned to the flat, where his meal was rapidly getting cold. And at 1.30 the first of the workmen (the team who knocked off at 12.30) were at the door wanting to be let in. So the afternoon progressed.

At 1.45 the building manager from regional office arrived to discuss progress with the foreman of the builders who were working on the Red Corridor. Not having been informed about this meeting, Chris was busy elsewhere, sorting out a store room in an area where he couldn't hear the persistent ringing of the door bell. In our flat, it was hard to ignore the deafening sound.

Realising eventually that Chris must be out of earshot, I stopped making pastry and opened a window, letting in the freezing air as I leaned out to explain why the caller was being kept waiting. My breath made clouds of mist as I offered to go and find Chris, who in Robert's absence was the only one with a key to the Green Door. I had no idea where in the vast house he might be, but after I had searched vainly in several areas some of the workmen eventually pointed me in the right direction and within a few minutes the building manager was, at last, inside the house; unfortunately, the builders' foreman, whom he had hoped to meet, was not. Nor had there been any message from him.

The building manager had another appointment and, under-standably annoyed, was obliged to leave.

The builders' foreman turned up ten minutes later – he had been delayed at another venue where he had other men to supervise. Whatever needed to be discussed between him and the building manager had to be delayed to another day. He, too, was looking rather tight-lipped as he departed.

At 2.30 p.m., the furniture restorer arrived, half an hour later than he had advised, to pick up some chairs which needed treatment. Chris had been hanging about in the cold, not wanting to be absent from the door when the bell rang and thus keep the restorer waiting. Though he was chilled and starting to feel irritable himself, he put on a pleasant face as he showed the man where the chairs were and helped him carry them out to his van.

The fog had thinned a little, allowing them to see a man, followed by his wife and three children, approaching through the front gate, which the restorer had left open.

"We were just driving by and saw the door open," the man said. "Are you open to the public? No? Oh, really? But the door's open! And we *are* members. Couldn't we just have a quick look round while we're here?"

Tactfully as he could, Chris explained that a "quick look round" really wasn't possible.

At 3.40, the architect and the contractor arrived to take a look at yet more dry rot which had been discovered in the stripped Morning Room. Whilst on the premises the architect took the opportunity to assess the progress of work on the shop and later advised Chris that the shop might not be fully ready to open at the end of March—cheering news to tell Robert when he returned.


Just when we thought the day was ending with the departure of the last workman at 6 o'clock, when the house had been walked for the final time, all doors closed and security systems in operation—then, as a final insult, the fire alarm blared out and sent us dashing to the panel.

Fortunately this was a false alarm, easily traced to a particular zone, where we were relieved to find there was no fire. However, the cause of the fault was not so easy to detect. A wisp of dust may activate a smoke detector, or there could be a fault in the equipment. On this occasion the problem was in one of the attics, where a detector was registering positive; it refused all efforts to persuade it that there was no smoke to be found.

The red light on the detector stayed on. At the panel, the buzzer kept on buzzing. Chris called the firm dealing with the fire system and their man on duty promised to come, though he couldn't reach Felbrigg before 9.

So we waited, snatching a meal in between keeping a watch on the alarm panel and checking the attics, while all the time the Hall grew colder and colder on a bitter winter's night. Nine o'clock arrived. The fire-alarm man didn't. It was nearer 10 o'clock before he appeared at last, having had a terrible journey from the city with freezing fog closing in again and an accident holding up traffic on the road. It took him three-quarters of an hour to fix the fault.

Just after 11, when Chris had re-checked the house and made sure all was secure for the night, he finally came up to the flat. He had been on duty with hardly a break since 7 a.m., managed to snatch two cups of coffee which were cold by the time he actually drank them, had an interrupted lunch lasting about twenty minutes in all, and a supper eaten while worrying about security. His adrenalin was still running high; to unwind, he watched television until the last dot disappeared after midnight, when he finally fell into bed exhausted.

And then in the small hours the fire alarm again blared its deafening wail, sounding loud enough to wake half the county. It was probably another false alarm, but still it had to be traced and checked, just in case. It was that same detector, its circuits still convinced that they could sense smoke. Chris disconnected it and, since risk of fire in that area was minimal, decided to leave it until morning. He needed some sleep. That early-bird painter was coming in again at 7.30!

## The Truth about Polishing

Having completed their long stint in the Library, the cleaners moved on through the upstairs dressing rooms and bedrooms, dusting walls and pictures, and polishing furniture.

Applying bees-wax polish is a once-yearly task, proud house-wives please note. Polish helps a duster to glide more easily but it does nothing for the wood; to feed and preserve the wood one must apply linseed oil. A thick coating of several layers of polish is actually harmful because the wood will be unable to 'breathe' and may dry out, unnoticed, beneath its apparent shine.

The truth of this was evidenced by the handrail on the main stair, which used to be so thick with polish that it felt tacky to the touch. Over time, the cleaners removed the built-up polish with applications of linseed oil and much elbow grease, and now the rail is smooth and warm, delightfully tactile as wood should be. Between annual polishings, fingermarks on woodwork are removed with a damp cloth rung out in special detergent, then the shine is brought back with a clean duster.

As the 'girls' go about their work they keep a sharp eye open for signs of woodworm, death-watch beetle, damp or other damage. They are all skilled at their job, following the rules of housekeeping laid down by the Trust's experts, using the special equipment provided, especially brushes—there are different brushes for every task, large and small, soft and bristly. Each cleaner carries a bag or basket containing her personal dusters and brushes, and each one knows her part in the routine. They are experienced enough to work without constant supervision, though in case of problems, or trouble discovered, they call in the houseman for help and advice.

The winter cleaning routine is hard work but, as all the ladies agree, very rewarding when they see the results.

## Secrets of the Ceilings

Meanwhile, working ahead on the high-level cleaning, Chris moved on to tackle the show rooms on the ground floor: the Cabinet, the Drawing Room, the Dining Room and the Great Hall. All of these rooms have decorative plaster ceilings, real dust-traps, and two of them—the Cabinet and the Drawing Room—are especially ornate, with leaves, fruit, game and intricate curlicues covering the entire area. The Drawing Room ceiling is three hundred years old—a real treasure—its date (1687), displayed in Roman numerals, forming part of the overall pattern.

Though in places the ceilings tend to look grey with the grime

The 'girls' arrive with their special brushes

of centuries, the only cleaning method allowed under Trust rules of housekeeping is the removal of dust. This requires the use of very soft brushes, of whatever size may be most appropriate; at the same time, but with the other hand, the operator is supposed to suck up the falling dust with a vacuum-cleaner crevice head which has been wrapped in foam rubber to protect the plaster-work from accidental knocks. The method is detailed in *The National Trust Manual of Housekeeping*.

The job is undertaken with the aid of a lightweight aluminium portable scaffold, an invaluable piece of equipment. Erecting it, fitting together the jig-saw of sections, involves an hour's work, but once up it can be wheeled about within a room and makes high-level work so much easier and safer than with hazardous ladders or steps.

Even with the aid of a scaffold, dusting old plaster ceilings, inch by intricate inch, can be a cold, lonely and physically taxing pastime. Arms ache from being held aloft; eyes start to strain in bad light; shoulders stiffen; hands are benumbed with cold; the vacuum head starts to weigh a ton and the vacuum cleaner itself takes up an unconscionable amount of room on the top of the scaffold where the operator is crouched. Application and self-motivation are vital if the houseman is to finish the job in time.

Finding the prescribed method somewhat awkward and unsatisfactory, Chris decided to use his ingenuity; on one of our Saturday outings to Norwich he bought a few yards of wine-maker's plastic pipe. This he taped to the crevice tool of a vacuum cleaner, forming a very fine vacuum head. Held between the fingers, alongside an over-sized artist's brush to do the dusting, the plastic pipe with its suction action provides the perfect instrument for removing and catching dust in one easy operation. And since the pipe is very light, and as long as one cares to make it, however high the operator has to work he can hold the brush and vacuum tube in one hand, leaving his other hand free to steady himself, while the heavy vacuum cleaner itself remains out of the way on the floor. It made life—and the tedious job—much easier.

Hearing about this newly-invented device, the head housekeeper sent a photographer to record Chris using it. He spent a whole day in the floodlit Drawing Room posing on top of the scaffold while pretending to use his vacuum pipe and brush on the chandelier. The result, blown up to poster-size, caused great excitement when one of our guides saw it displayed at a Trust exhibition.

The room called the Cabinet has another intricate ceiling, burgeoning with fruit and flowers, all linked by fronds and leafy tendrils. This room is one of the most splendid at Felbrigg; one imagines the gentlemen withdrawing there with their brandy and cigars for after-dinner conversation. Its walls are lined with crimson worsted damask which sets off the magnificent collection of pictures brought home by William Windham II as souvenirs of his Grand Tour through Europe. Windham had the room remodelled in order to exhibit his collection, which he displayed in matching gilded frames. A treasured possession of Felbrigg is the 'picture-hang' diagrams of all four walls, designed by Windham II himself; his pictures still hang where he planned they should go.

The furniture is wonderfully rich and ornate, especially the two Boulle desks—inlaid with brass and tortoiseshell worked together in a gleaming red and gold pattern of pictures and shapes.

However, since it faces north, the Cabinet is one of the darkest and coldest rooms in the house. In winter its gloom is only slightly lightened by two table lamps, its freezing chill scarcely alleviated by a small blow heater. But it was there, on an afternoon when Chris was employed on cleaning the ceiling, all on his own in the silent, shadowed house with the furniture shrouded in dust sheets, that there occurred one of the magical moments which now and then unexpectedly punctuate the humdrum routine.

He was high up on the scaffolding tower with his new vacuum pipe and brush, right near the ceiling, cleaning plasterwork which is fashioned into vine tendrils and leaves, flowers, buds, floral shoots. All at once he fancied he saw a little face peering at him among the other shapes. Two tiny eyes, ears, a snout . . . it was a pig! Wasn't it? Could it be?

This was a 'flowers and fruit only' ceiling—or so everyone believed. But as he looked more closely, following the artistic logic of the pattern, he made out other animal faces—a hawk, a monkey, a fox, a walrus?!—eight of them altogether, placed at intervals around the centrepiece of the ceiling, all at the same regular junction of leafy tendrils. In great excitement, he called me down from the flat to see if I too could make out the faces. I could, given careful instructions where to look, and with a torch for a spotlight; they were most definitely animal heads, cunningly hidden among the fruit and foliage.

The faces are visible only from very close to; someone standing on the floor beneath has to be very sharp-eyed to see the faces even when they're pointed out. Chris delighted in revealing his discovery to our team of guides, some of whom have been with the house for many years, but none of whom had spotted this evidence of what we guess was probably a joke perpetrated by the master-plasterers, Joseph Rose and George Green, who in the mid-eighteenth century altered this ceiling under instructions from architect James Paine.

The secret animals on the ceiling

## Cleaning the Chandeliers

Another winter job—which summer visitors often ask about—is the cleaning of the chandeliers. Chris sometimes informs enquirers that this is done by taking the chandeliers on to the lawn and hosing them down. Occasionally they believe him.

We have two chandeliers at Felbrigg (one is actually a gasolier complete with taps and glass gas pipes). The aim is to clean both each year, though there is not always time to accomplish this feat. This is another team effort, employing the houseman and all of the cleaners. It may take two days to complete each chandelier.

To save time, Chris spent one Sunday evening moving the dust-sheeted furniture aside to create space in the Drawing Room. Then he erected the scaffolding under the chandelier, and brought in trestle tables, so that the cleaning of the chandelier could begin as soon as the ladies arrived on Monday morning.

They all assembled in the Drawing Room, where politician William Windham III looks sternly down from over the mantel. Bowls of warm water were brought, one laced with a special detergent used by the Trust; cloths and towels were readied, and a sheet laid on the floor for the laying-out of the crystal drops. The cleaners put on their rubber gloves; Chris was wearing white cotton ones. All was ready.

Three of the ladies arranged themselves by the trestle table; the fourth stood by to fetch and carry while Chris climbed the scaffold and carefully unhooked the first piece of crystal. He laid it in the cupped hands of the youngest and most active of the cleaners, who took it to the table, where the first of her colleagues washed it, gently removing the film of dust which had accumulated. The second lady then rinsed it; the third dried it and placed it carefully on a dry cloth on the table. Soon a rhythm was established, crystal drops moving on a human conveyor belt, down from the chandelier, through the cleaning process and finally being laid in careful order on the sheet on the floor.

Inevitably, as with all such operations, unexpected snags caused delays. The chandeliers are old. Some of the tiny brass hooks which hold the crystals were worn and apt to break; they had to be fixed before the pendants were replaced. Some had obviously broken in previous years and the make-shift repairs didn't work properly. Bent pins had been used, which had now rusted. Each pendant, as it came down, had to be examined for wear and tear, handled carefully so as not to create further damage.

Care also had to be taken to keep a note of each set of pieces and where it belonged in the overall pattern. There are small drops with only one or two crystals, longer links of four or five, and many long, heavy 'necklaces' with twenty-five crystal drops gleaming like huge diamonds. A chandelier is like a three-dimensional jig-saw; should the pieces become jumbled, rebuilding the picture correctly will be a nightmare. To avoid this problem, the job must be done slowly and methodically.

By noon, when the ladies stopped work for the day, the chandelier was two-thirds stripped. They left the room as it was, locking the door so that no one would disturb the crystals, and Chris spent the afternoon applying himself to ceiling-cleaning in the Dining Room next door.

At nine the next morning, fresh bowls of water were brought to the Drawing Room and the job resumed. Finally, when the gilt skeleton of the chandelier was denuded of its crystal gown, it too had to be cleaned, wiped free of dust and cobwebs, and the glass wax-catchers beneath each candle-holder had to be washed.

When all was done, then carefully one by one the glittering drops were replaced. The cleaners brought them to the scaffold, where Chris with aching arms hung the crystals back on their tiny hooks, building up the chandelier to its former glory. But now it shone, gleaming even in winter half-light that struck rainbows from each facet, a glorious sight that made all the hard work worth while. A delighted Chris called me to come and see.

Just looking at a freshly washed chandelier, sharing delight in its beauty along with the cleaners who helped accomplish the miracle, is one of the pleasures that are part of our life with the Trust.

## The New Restaurant

With the high-level cleaning coming to a conclusion, the ladies could now occupy themselves with the walls, furniture and carpets of the main ground floor state rooms. The cleaning, at least, was running pretty well to schedule.

Meanwhile . . .

With builders still in the corridor and shop, and others in the

Morning Room, another project got underway—the tea-room was to be turned into a fully functioning restaurant.

In the comparatively short time since the house had been in the care of the National Trust, preservation and essential maintenance of the fabric and contents had been a priority. This year, however, precious funds had been allocated to the improvement of the tea-room. Until then, very light snacks such as soup and a roll, or tea and scones, had been served from a long table in the Old Kitchen.

The tea-room area comprises three rooms. The Old Kitchen itself is enormous, with a very high ceiling; its tall arched windows overlook a grass courtyard. One wall is hung with old copper pans and other antique equipment, fish kettles and preserving pans. Where the huge fireplace used to be there now stands an Aga cooker. When we arrived there was also a toaster and a hot plate used by the tea-room ladies, and a deep stone sink for washing up, while against the window wall was an anonymous built-in feature about the same size as the Aga, a sort of brick table, covered in formica and used as an extra work-surface; it was thought to have been a 'coal-store'—a storage place for solid fuel in the days when open fires were in use for cooking.

On the stone flag floor of the kitchen stood a few tables and chairs for the convenience of visitors, with overflow seating in a smaller ante-room next door, which had once been the housekeeper's sitting room. Next to that was a cramped 'still room' complete with deep sinks and huge cupboards—this room was used mainly by the cleaners and by the lady who did the flowers, being the only convenient source of water in the main Hall.

The plan was to turn the still room into a kitchen/preparation area and the ante-room into a servery, leaving the Old Kitchen itself as the restaurant. This would entail the removal of the big old sink and the 'coal-store' in the main room; the erection of a serving counter in the ante-room; and the installation of cookers, fridges and so forth in the still room.

Before any work could go ahead the architect had to give his final okay and the historic buildings representative had to be happy that the essential ambience of the old house was not being spoiled; no radical changes to structure are allowed, for instance fireplaces cannot be removed, though they may be covered or disguised. Even the colour of paint on the walls can be the subject of much argument and deliberation; the Trust tries hard to keep the historical integrity of its properties intact.

Members of the support staff from regional office, with the building contractor, and the administrator, had met on site several times to discuss exactly what should be done and when. Now, at last, the work was to begin. Could the new restaurant possibly be ready by the end of March?

The alterations brought yet another team of workmen to the house, all needing to be let in and out, all needing to be checked from time to time. If not watched they were prone to wander about, like Alice in Wonderland driven by curiosity to try doors and get into places they shouldn't be.

Apart from physical upheaval, extra noise and dust, and more workmen, the making of the restaurant brought other new faces to the house. The post of manager/ess had to be filled; applicants came for interview and a lady named Joan was chosen. A catering expert also came to inspect the venue and give advice; she called back two or three times at various stages of the alterations. And since the new restaurant had to be licensed there were meetings with a solicitor and the fire officer, who ensured that fire regulations would be obeyed. All of these visits had to be co-ordinated and fitted in with the other work that was going on.

At times the house, large as it is, seemed to be full of people all doing different things, and all making separate demands. However, except at inevitable moments when strength and spirits drooped, we managed to ride the problems with sanguinity. The new restaurant would allow us to offer better facilities to our visitors—that was the main object of all efforts.


Among the many clearing-up jobs which still kept Chris occupied most evenings and weekends, several dozen heavy boxes of books had to be moved from the shop store room to a new store above, entailing many journeys up and down a narrow, winding wooden stairway. I naturally offered to help; the job took the two of us a whole Saturday afternoon.

We also spent a good deal of time sorting out the 'lock-up' area, a labyrinth of dank, gloomy rooms on two floors, at the end of a wing never seen by the public. The lock-up actually does contain a room with barred windows—reputedly once used to restrain poachers caught on the estate. However, the whole warren was piled with generations of discarded household accoutrements and equipment: lead pipes and marble slabs, old grates and slates, bath surrounds, Victorian dining chairs that were falling to pieces, ancient safes, and the back and two legs of a William and Mary chair—evidently part of a set, three of which are still on show in the staircase hall. This part-chair is painted, which makes us wonder if it was the fashion to have such furniture painted and not stripped and stained as are the three remaining chairs. Another really intriguing find was a metal chest, threatened with rust, which at first we could not identify. But more of that later.

Chris and Robert were gradually clearing one area of the lock-up to create space for new deep freezers for the restaurant, hopefully leaving a few square yards to provide a work-room for Chris—had he continued to do the never-ending carpentry, painting and mending jobs in our flat it might have ended in divorce.

## The Ice-House

It was still bitterly cold, with flurries of snow and days of icy rain relieved by an hour here and there when the sun shone. Outside in the park, work began on laying a new septic tank. Mechanical diggers started cutting a pit, leaving giant molehills of soil on the grass. When the tank itself arrived it stood for a few days beside its ready grave, a great fat shape that was swiftly christened 'The Pig'. Later, the gardeners would reseed the bare earth and in a few weeks' time, when the first visitors of the season arrived, nothing would show in the pasture but a couple of man-hole covers.

There were still many parts of the estate that we had not had time to see, though we were slowly expanding our knowledge. Having been told that there was an old ice-house in the woods, on one of our free days we took a walk to find it. It lies up the slope behind the house, alongside one of the broad 'rides' which form a great V shape between swathes of conifers mixed with beech. This area, once a sandy heath between the deer park and the Great Wood, is now called Victory Wood—it was planted as a memorial to VE Day at the end of the Second World War. (The last squire's younger brother served in the Royal Air Force and was killed in Crete during the war; the seat at the apex of the 'Victory V' walk bears a dedicatory plaque.)

At first sight, the ice-house itself might be a relic of that same war; its rounded hummock is not unlike an air-raid shelter, hidden in summer under a growth of grasses, moss and small shrubs. Lying under the shade of tall trees, it may easily go unremarked unless you know it's there. Uneven steps lead down to a cage-like door, now barred and padlocked, beyond which

The ice-house in the woods

lies echoing darkness. You will need a torch to take a proper look at the round arched roof, which is a miracle of the brick-layer's art, and to peer down into the twenty-eight-foot brick-lined pit half choked with leaves.

We are still rather curious as to how exactly this ice-house was used; the lake, from where presumably the ice had to come, is a good half mile away, and the ice-house itself is remote from the Hall—a long walk for whichever servant was sent to fetch the meat. However, we understand that it's quite possible that snow was used rather than ice, and that whole carcasses were sometimes stored in the ice-house. It's said that the ice in that deep dark hole could last as long as two years.

(There is also a rumour that many years ago when the ice-house was cleaned out a workman found a revolver which belonged to the wife of the then squire. Oh, intrigue—the imagination runs wild!)

As a bonus on that bright, bitter day, we discovered snowdrops sheltering under trailing bramble briars, and in the Orangery, built in 1705, the first camellias were budding, perfect pink waxy blooms streaked with delicate red and white, tightly-furled as yet. In the depths of February, such signs of spring were very welcome.


## Felbrigg Throws a Party

One of the land agents from regional office was leaving. He had evinced a particular fondness for Felbrigg, especially the Dining Room; Robert was asked to organise a farewell party in that room. Despite his protests that given the present condition of the house, with all the repairs in progress, a party for thirty or forty people would mean an enormous amount of extra work for himself and Chris, regional office insisted. The party was to take place on a Friday.

Apart from containing its own furniture, all under wraps, the Dining Room was the repository for most of the furniture and accoutrements stripped from the Morning Room. It was crammed to capacity with pictures and tables, chairs, bureaux, porcelain and glassware, not to mention the heavy roll of the Morning Room carpet. All of these precious objects had to be moved and stored safely out of the way in some convenient space before the room could be made ready for the party.

That week Chris worked all hours in between routine jobs to clear the Dining Room. Anyone available was called in to help —mainly me, plus our son Kevin and a friend of his, who both dropped in to see us one evening, hoping for a meal, and found themselves co-opted to the cause. Actually they seemed to relish the privilege of being admitted 'behind the scenes'. Certainly we were glad of their strength and energy. Item by item, the Dining Room was cleared, larger furniture being carefully eased through the doorway into the staircase hall, smaller pieces taken to the adjacent Drawing Room, which was of course still draped in dust sheets in common with all the show rooms, though its chandelier, newly cleaned, glinted rainbows in the gloaming left by closed shutters.

Sixteen leather dining chairs and two armchairs were removed, too, and the porcelain and glass from the side tables. In accordance with Trust practice, everything had to be carried in a special way. If moving porcelain or glass, only one piece at a time must be carried. Only responsible people are allowed to move delicate objects.

Finally, the huge table was dismantled and moved to one side to act as a buffet for the party; it would be covered in thick layers of baize and protective plastic sheeting, topped with a white tablecloth. This was, after all, one of our main show rooms and we had to take every precaution to guard its contents.

Because our own in-house catering was not yet adequate to the task, an outside caterer had been booked. Unfortunately the young lady concerned arrived at the last minute expecting all kinds of facilities which were not available, but worst of all she brought a calor-gas stove on which to prepare curried prawns —and it's a strict rule that naked flames are not allowed inside the mansion except under the closest supervision. She was eventually allowed to proceed on condition that she kept a fire extinguisher close by, though she evidently felt we were making a big fuss about nothing.

In the end, despite the headaches, the party took place with no real problems. Nobody spilled wine on the precious carpet and the caterer didn't, after all, set fire to the kitchen.

When the revellers had gone, near midnight, some clearing up needed to be done before we could settle the house for the night, and over the following weekend the Dining Room carpet had to be vacuum-cleaned, and all the furniture—including the extra pieces from the Morning Room—replaced, so that normal work could resume as usual first thing on Monday.

## Of Mice and . . .

Now well into harness after nearly three months, among all his other jobs—including Chief of Security, Fire Chief, Doorbell-Answerer, Cleaning Supremo, Mr Shifter, Drain-Clearer Designate, Workman Watcher, Clerk-Typist, Head Handyman etc. etc.—Chris had been appointed Lord High Rodent Exterminator. Since the tea-room had finished serving teas at Christmas and we had distributed all the left-over buns and scones to the sea-birds at one of the reservations along the coast, the inevitable mice lurking in cavities and attics had been searching further afield for food. Traps were left in strategic places. Several summary executions had taken place.

With builders in the Old Kitchen, the only place the mice could find food was in the private flats. Robert reported that Sam, his bull-terrier, was fascinated by little furry friends who ran across his kitchen floor, and we frequently heard scratchings in our own ceilings and behind the skirtings. We were careful to keep our food cupboards well protected.

More welcome wildlife came in the shape of birds visiting our windowsills—great-tits, coal-tits, cheeky blue-tits with their funny crew-cuts; chaffinches, green finches; even a jay or two (rarely anything so mundane as a sparrow or a starling). The blue-tits, especially, would come and rap on the window if we were tardy in putting out their scraps. Delighted by these charming and amusing visitors, we collected spare fat, bacon rinds and stale cake, and bought an enormous bag of wild-bird food, putting out a supply each day. We kept the rest of the bird food in a small waste-bin in a corner of our bedroom—the nearest point to the 'bird' window.

But birds are not the only ones who like seeds and crunchy tidbits. One night I was reading in bed when I heard a rustling. Large as life, a mouse jumped into the bin of bird food, helped himself and scurried away. Luckily I'm not afraid of mice; I found this one's cheekiness rather amusing. But the joke went a bit flat when, a night or two later, I threw back the bed covers and that same (well, presumably the same) mouse jumped out from between the pillows! This meant war. More traps were set.

## Inside Information

Towards the end of our closed season, on two or three occasions, one meeting a week, our room wardens gather to hear their peers expound on favourite subjects connected with the Hall. One volunteer is an expert on the Library; one has built up a detailed knowledge of the history and contents of the Great Hall; another delights in 'oddment' stories about all manner of things to do with the house. And as a special treat Chris may give a 'pot pourri' talk showing some of the precious and unusual things, culled from cupboards and attics, which he has discovered. There is some delicate glassware, including a set of tiny drinking glasses shaped like four-leafed clovers, shimmering with rainbow colours—they're beautiful but they don't look easy to drink from—and two tiny decanters with long elegant tops, decorated with gold. Then there are the curios: the helmet of a militiaman; an ostrich egg carved and painted; a toy taxi still in lovely condition; dance cards with their pencils attached and names filled in (some rather sparse, so that one feels for the poor wallflowers); Christmas cards and Valentines; a mourning ring. . . . Sadly, at present it's impossible for us to put these treasures on permanent show because of lack of space and suitable display points.

Our room stewards are delightful people. Mostly retired, they come from all walks of life and they take an enormous interest in the Hall and its doings. Their winter visits mean opening up and heating rooms (and lavatories) not routinely in use, preserving security while they're here, and closing down after them, but we are glad to see them come for their meetings. The winter seems very quiet without them.

Corridor lampshades, lanterns and their environs were the next priority for the houseman, with the help of the scaffolding in the case of some high-ceilinged areas. The cleaners had finished their basic chores in the main rooms and were also starting in the corridors, after which they would be cleaning bronzes and polishing the copper utensils which hang in the Old Kitchen.

With only four weeks left in which to prepare for the fray, much remained to be done and there were still three sets of workmen busy inside the house—in the shop and corridor, in the restaurant, and in the Morning Room—with consequent dirt, noise and comings and goings continuing. Would any of them be finished in time?

As we envisaged the possibility of opening amid chaos, Felbrigg decided to keep us amused with a plague of fire-alarm faults. Various buzzers and bells kept going off at all hours. Every time the alarm sounded, Robert and Chris dropped whatever they were doing (or roused from a warm bed) and hurried to the source of the trouble. After eight such disturbances in a week, the engineer was called in to check the system thoroughly. Tracing and eliminating various gremlins took him two full days.

A hundred and one small occurrences continued to fill up the slightest gap in the working routine. Various photographers came, including one sent by the Victoria and Albert Museum to take pictures of some rococo mirrors and wall brackets which we were lending for an exhibition later in the year; newly painted notice boards arrived ready for the coming season; a plumber fixed leaks in the roof—with a blow-torch, causing Chris to visit him every hour to make sure he hadn't started a fire; oh, and British Telecom were in for three weeks fixing a whole new phone system with extensions in several useful places such as the shop, the tea-room and our flat. That tale alone would fill another chapter.

To add variety, there were problems with the plumbing. In such an old house the pipes and wiring are a miracle of confusion; Chris spent hours, between other jobs, in the attics and relevant voids between floors, becoming festooned in dusty cobwebs. He was building a picture of what pipe led where and which tank fed what system, the better to deal with future troubles.

Somehow, during the course of these investigations, the heavy door of the ladies' lavatory slammed shut on his thumb. The thumb swelled up and was very painful, necessitating a trip to Cromer hospital, where confusion was caused by the patient's stated occupation. The doctor seemed strangely affable and forthcoming until he discovered that in this case a 'houseman' was not a junior hospital doctor but literally a man who looked after a house. Our hero spent the next week or two sporting a 'spiker' bandage and a very sore thumb. His completely truthful explanation—that he broke the thumb in the ladies' loo—gave rise to predictable ribaldry.

## The Base Camp

An extra facility at Felbrigg is a 'base camp'—not for the benefit of mountaineers, not in Norfolk; no, this base camp is a place where groups can base themselves to eat and sleep while they do work for the Trust or take a holiday in our area. Young National Trust groups come to stay from time to time at an 'Acorn Camp' to help with projects in woods and parks locally; they might build steps on sloping pathways, or clear undergrowth. But the base camp is available at other times to anyone who cares to hire it—scout groups, church groups, students. . . .

This basic accommodation is situated on the first floor of the stable block. It comprises a central area of kitchen, dining room and lounge set between two dormitories, each of which is designed to sleep ten people. There are toilets and showers, plus a double-bedded room for the group leader.

Before the season began, the base camp had to be cleaned and checked to make sure everything was working correctly and there would be no problems for our first campers. The inventory was updated, fire orders amended, notices brought up to date. The wintry weather had caused leaks in the water pipes, which only showed themselves when the water was turned on, so a plumber was summoned, waited for and directed to the scene of the problem.

The base camp is another source of complications for house staff, even when it's empty. When it's inhabited . . . but we'll go into that when the time comes.

## Spring Walks

A guided walk through the spring-budding woods was led by the head forester for the region. About forty people had bought tickets and when they gathered in the car park I joined them, eager to know more of our surroundings. Most of us were warmly wrapped and sturdily shod, some old hands carrying walking sticks. Those who had come less well equipped were soon having to dodge and tiptoe round puddles and patches of thick wet mud as we made our way deeper into the woods, pausing every now and then while the forester explained the history of the trees and the Trust's policy on planting and conservation.

Felbrigg's woods and parkland are especially interesting to the connoisseur. Down through the generations, several owners of the house have taken a deep interest in planting trees. It is thought, too, that part of the park may have been planned by the young Humphry Repton, who lived nearby, before he really began on his brilliant career as a landscaper. In spring, as the trees unfurl their leaves, an amazing number of different greens show themselves. There are oaks and sycamore, enormous beeches, and ancient sweet chestnuts, all gnarled and twisted, their trunks like vast corkscrews, winding tighter as they grow older. They always remind me of the Ents, the tree-folk of Tolkien's Middle Earth.

Loving trees as I do, I find the woods endlessly enchanting. They are a continual source of uplift and consolation, their loveliness changing with the seasons, helping to soothe us in some of the more difficult moments. While walking, we may see many kinds of beautiful birds—apart from the ubiquitous blackbirds and robins there are blue-tits, coal-tits, great-tits; chaffinches and green finches; colourful jays with their white rumps as they fly away; pheasants croak and clatter away in alarm, grouse and red-legged partridge dot the fields; geese of the Brent and Canadian varieties graze on the pasture. Two pairs of Egyptian geese nest in a tree in the park; pied wagtails make our courtyard their strutting ground, and as the year goes on the cuckoos will arrive, and after them dozens of martins and swallows will rear their young under the eaves of the Hall. Animals too live nearby: grey squirrels dart about and vanish up trees, and we may be vouchsafed a glimpse of a fox or even, though rarely, a deer.

However, one particular spring walk proved less than idyllic. On a mild Sunday afternoon, Chris and I took a stroll in the gardens. We didn't go far from the house since Chris was on duty, it being Robert's turn to have a weekend off, but the weather was too pleasant to miss the chance of a walk in the fresh air. Several other people were about; there were a few cars in the car park, belonging to people who were enjoying the park, or the lakeside or the woodland walk—all of which are open all year round.

As we strolled, we spotted two middle-aged women entering the gardens by a back way from the woods. To reach that point they must have come right through an area whose pathways are barriered and clearly marked 'Private—No Entry'. When they saw us, one woman appeared about to turn back but the other held her ground.

"Excuse me," Chris greeted, "did you know we are closed until the end of the month?"

The spokeswoman answered stiffly: "What about it?"

Two middle-aged lady trespassers

"You're quite welcome to walk in the woods, or the park," he replied, "but the gardens are closed to visitors until the end of the month. You must have come right past the 'Private' sign in the woods. Didn't you see it?"

"Of course we did. We live locally. We come through here all the time."

"You mean," was the polite but pointed reply, "you often come through the private area of the woods and get into the gardens when you know we're closed?"

The lady was turning defensive and losing her temper. Though her companion looked embarrassed and began to murmur apologies, her voice was drowned by the angry words of her friend: 'You people are all the same. You think you own the place."

"I just work here," Chris said. "I'm sorry, but the gardens are closed. I must ask you to go back the way you came."

Since there was no point in standing and arguing, we moved away. The lady yelled after us, "You're no better than a Nazi You ought to be wearing a swastika! You're all the same, you people! 'Heil, Hitler! Heil, Hitler!'"

## The Quickening of the Year

In the orangery several varieties of camellia were in bloom— pink, scarlet and cream—while in clumps across the park in front of the house daffodils began to bud. By Easter they would provide a glorious golden show as visitors walked the approach path. Trees and shrubs were budding, too, and birds were busy nest-building, filling the air with their mating songs. Spring was on the way.

So was our first day of opening.

An essential gathering at this time of year is the pre-season meeting for all house staff. This is one of only two occasions in the year when our volunteer room wardens have the chance to meet *en masse* and mingle with other seasonal employees who will be working in the restaurant and shop. It's a time for old friends to swap gossip and for new acquaintances to be made That year there were many new faces. All of the management team would be starting fresh to the Open season at Felbrigg— Robert and Chris, Joan in the restaurant and Peter in the shop Robert invited me to attend the meeting, too; however unofficial and ill-defined my role, I had become an integral part of the Felbrigg scene.

This was also the time to pass on news about happenings in the house, and for the duties of room guides to be reiterated. For security reasons, photography was no longer to be allowed inside the house; visitors who missed the sign at the entrance were to be politely dissuaded from taking snaps. And, as always, no one should handle furniture, glass, porcelain, books or fabrics however tempted. Those curtains are a hundred and fifty year old and already flaking and friable; that piece of porcelain might have been recently mended, or this glass stopper could be at the point of breaking. Imagine the damage fifty thousand fingers could cause in just one season.

The strict 'don't touch' rule applies equally, and for the same reason, to room wardens. They should not open drawers or cabinets, or lift objects, even if visitors request it. A room warden's primary function is security. Talking about the rooms, answering questions and supplying extra information to visitors, rewarding though that can be, is not a requisite of the job.

Everyone seemed to enjoy the pre-season meeting, though that first year it was daunting for us meeting so many new faces. We had seen many of the room wardens before, at the Christmas party when we were very new to Felbrigg, and on the occasions of the guides' talks, but now we were all meeting as a team, new staff and old hoping to blend together to bring about a successful season. The mood of renewal and hope filled the Morning Room almost tangibly. We were all looking forward to the coming months.

By that time the Morning Room had been restored to its elegant self, with floorboards and painted panelling being replaced. An expert painter had repaired slight damage to the panelling, unavoidably caused when it was taken down from the wall. Blending his new paintwork with the old had been painstaking work which had made him a regular presence for about two weeks.

The new restaurant was also taking shape, though as yet it was nowhere near completion. The Old Kitchen, where visitors would take refreshments, was more or less ready, but work was still going on in the new kitchen and the servery. When the self-service counter arrived it had to be brought in through the window—it was too long to be manoeuvred round the corridors and passageways from the back door. Getting it into place was another performance of skill and care for Chris and the workmen. Nearly every day new cookers, fridges, freezers and various smaller appliances were delivered. Space had to be found in the lock-up for them to be stored out of the way while the workmen completed the building work.

Before the servery and kitchen could be brought into proper use, both rooms had to be replastered, decorated, and have new flooring laid. It seemed unlikely that they could be properly ready by the end of the month. Joan reluctantly resigned herself to providing only a minimum service to our first visitors.

One job that could now be tackled, though, was the cleaning of the flagstoned expanses of the Old Kitchen floor. For this job the house possesses an enormous electric scrubbing machine, which is extremely heavy and wilful. It takes all a man's strength to keep it from flying off in directions of its own choosing. Care must be taken not to wet the floor too much, otherwise the flags will be encouraged to flake.

Certain areas of the floor, which had been under coconut matting, were badly stained and soiled. Chris ran the machine over these areas several times, allowing them to dry in between, trying different sorts of detergent which all churned into brown sludge as the dirt lifted. The operation took several days to complete.

Now the copper, gleaming from the attentions of the cleaners, could be rehung on the wall, and Joan could plan her arrangement of tables and chairs. It was beginning to look like a restaurant at last, even if—sadly—it wouldn't be fully in use by March 31st.

Neither, it appeared, would the shop be entirely ready when we opened, but Peter, its newly-appointed manager, would be able to use part of it. He was in the shop frequently, taking deliveries of goods from the National Trust central depot and storing them in his stock room as he began to dress his displays. Soon the familiar scent of herbs and soaps, which makes every National Trust shop such a pleasure to visit, was spreading through the air, wafting into the corridor. We could feel the place beginning to come to life again.

## Another Discovery

During the re-organisation of the kitchen, the house had another surprise to reveal: when workmen began to dismantle the so-called 'coal store', by removing its wooden top, they discovered, not the flat brick top they expected but a very old type of stove, with square and rectangular metal 'baskets' set into the brickwork. The whole thing was filthy with the detritus of ages, but a little brushing revealed cemented channels lying underneath the baskets, ingeniously-shaped flues through which ash could drop to the floor at the front of the stove. The openings through which the debris was once collected, probably by the lowly 'backus boy', had been bricked up at some time.

Enchanted by the discovery, after the workmen left that evening, Chris and I set about cleaning up the stove, clearing the flues by means of a vacuum cleaner. We consulted our reference books and found that what had been uncovered was most probably a 'stewing stove', dating from the seventeenth century. The metal baskets were intended to hold glowing charcoal which would gently simmer the contents of saucepans and stew-pots sitting on top. In effect, the stove is an early barbecue.

The cleaners too were most interested in the discovery and soon applied black-lead to its top, restoring it nearer to its original appearance. The Trust's historical experts agreed that the stove was much too important a feature to be taken out. It remains on view in the refurbished restaurant, a great talking point for visitors.

## Setting up for Opening

The time arrived when the cleaners could begin to set up the rooms again. First comes the removal of the dust covers, some of which are voluminous—imagine the size of dust sheets covering a four-poster bed, for instance. They have to be taken down with care, sometimes needing the assistance of the houseman; the furniture has ornate curlicues and delicate decorations that must not be damaged. When finally the sheets are down they are neatly folded and stored away for use next year; then the room is reinstated, chairs, tables, and towel rails replaced as appropriate. If heavy objects such as bronzes have to be moved, the houseman is again called in to lend his muscle. Bed and chair covers are spread and smoothed; many of them are white cotton and have been laundered, starched and ironed to pristine finish. Then the final smaller items are brought out of safe-keeping—clocks, silver candlesticks, toilette articles, glassware and books are arranged to dress the rooms.

At Felbrigg, the idea is that the house should look and feel like a home, not a museum. That's what the last owner intended and we try to respect his wishes. The cleaners love to restore the rooms to their shining, orderly, on-show state. It is the culmination of their winter's work, a reward at the end of long hours in dark, cold rooms doing often unpleasant and tedious jobs.

We share their delight. We could not manage without our invaluable 'girls'.

When the rooms are almost ready, the houseman can begin to set up and wind all the clocks. This can be a lengthy job and calls for skill and patience, especially with some long-case monsters which need fine balancing. There are many different time-pieces, some small and ornate, bright with ormolu or enamelling, others eight feet tall; some sit on mantels and tables, others stand in corridors and in hallways. A particular treasure of Felbrigg is the Tompion bracket clock which is displayed on the Boulle desk in the Drawing Room. Its case is ebony, with brass panels chased and engraved, and it was made by a famous clockmaker who practised his craft during the late seventeenth century. It has been said that Thomas Tompion's clocks were unsurpassed for accuracy until the digital clock came along.

Some of the clocks have been away during the winter, under the care of specialists, but they now come home to the places which wait for them. With all of them restored to life the house begins to waken from its long sleep; the hours are marked by swift silver chimes and stately bronze strokes, a charming chorus ringing through hushed rooms. Keeping them going during the season is another of the houseman's jobs; he winds the clocks once a week—all of them, with one exception.

That exception is the courtyard clock which stands high over the east wing of the house. Its heavy mechanism is wound throughout the year by Tom, our head woodsman, who twice every week climbs the winding, dusty stairs through cobwebs and gloom to perform his task. The courtyard clock strikes every hour, but though it can be heard clearly from our flat it never keeps us awake. It's a regular feature of Felbrigg that is sadly missed by residents on the rare occasions when it has to be stopped for repair.

Another touch that visitors may not notice—but we do—is the placing of fresh candles in wall sconces, candelabra and chandeliers at the beginning of the season. It's difficult to get the right sort of long white candles but Chris solved the problem by getting in touch with a church supplier and placing an order. Since there are so many candles in the Hall, fitting them in their sockets is a time-consuming task involving step-ladders; an obliging wife may be called in to stand by and judge when each candle is perfectly upright.

Also in the final run-down before opening, there were ropes to hang, to mark the visitors' route through the rooms; notice boards to fix in various places; a menu board to make for the new restaurant; new fire orders to type out for the guides' folders, and lamps and heaters to be checked.

Another vital area, which could not be forgotten in the rush to prepare the more glamorous apartments, was the guides' tea-room.

Many of our volunteers are elderly; all of them give freely of their time. They deserve a pleasant break during their four hours' work, so their private tea-room—actually a disused bathroom still complete with bath—is now set up with kettle, cups and saucers, spoons, sugar, biscuits, washing-up liquid, mop and clean tea-towels. Everything in the room must be clean and fresh. If it isn't just so, someone will soon tell us; our room wardens are very particular!

On the last day before we opened, the cleaners did a final run through, dusting and vacuum-cleaning as they would continue to do every open day during the season (except Saturday, their day off). As they went, they checked that everything was as it should be and if they noticed anything undone or out of place they alerted Chris to the fact. There were a hundred and one small jobs for him to do at this stage, but at the end of a busy day he found satisfaction and pleasure in walking through the house and seeing that all was ready.

At least . . . it was ready except that the restaurant wouldn't be fully in operation, the shop was able to use only half its capacity, and there were still workmen in the Red Corridor. Hey, ho!

# 3

# Spring—The Opening Season

### Our Very First 'Open' Day

By the time our first 'open' day arrived, daffodils were nodding on the pasture fronting the House, the camellias in the Orangery were a vision of waxy pinks, creams and reds against the shiny dark leaves of eighty-year-old trees, and in the walled garden the magnificent collection of hawthorn trees was beginning to blossom. Spring at Felbrigg is a sight to behold.

Despite the chaos still evident behind the scenes, we were all eager to start the season.

On the last Saturday in March, Chris was about before 7.30, snatching a quick cup of coffee before going down to open the house. This entailed moving through every room and corridor, unlocking doors with various keys, and opening the shutters which guard every window. Usually the blinds are left down at this point: too much daylight is damaging. If all goes well, barring accidents and unforeseen complications, opening up at Felbrigg takes about forty minutes.

By the time Chris came for breakfast I, too, was up and about. Our younger son, Kevin, and his friend Steve, who were both staying with us for a couple of days, remained in their beds, surfacing later as youths will.

The workmen had departed at 6 o'clock the previous night, leaving piles of rubble. The restaurant and corridors were filthy, floors and dustsheets covered in thick gritty dust, though at least the flagstones had been replaced over the drainage channels so that no gaping holes remained to trap unwary visitors.

Even though it was a Saturday, Debbie, the youngest of the four cleaners, had volunteered to come in especially to help get the place finally ready. Though she was a willing worker there was too much for her to cope with alone. While she did more routine cleaning elsewhere, Chris swept up the mess left by the workmen and removed the mounds of rubble before taking off the dust sheets and shaking them outside. Meanwhile, I was typing notices of apology, explaining the reasons for our half-open shop and tea-room. When I went down with these, I found myself enlisted to help with the cleaning of the corridor. Kevin and Steve appeared, curious to see what was happening. They too were drafted into service.

The broad windowsills—seven of them—plus all the glazing bars, were covered in grit that I washed off while Debbie vacuum-cleaned the entire length of the stone corridor. The boys made themselves useful shaking out and beating doormats in the grass courtyard behind the house. Then Debbie and I set about washing all the windows, which are very tall, cover a large area and are composed of small panes—cleaning them was a long, fiddly task. Meanwhile Chris and the boys brought in some of the furniture—the chests, tables and chairs which make the corridor more friendly. There were notices to be arranged on notice boards, brochures and guides to be positioned at the entrance, and the ticket desk to be prepared—to name only the main essentials.

We finished in time to grab lunch around 1 o'clock, so that Chris was ready to do the final raising of blinds and checking of all the rooms before the volunteer wardens began to arrive.

That day Robert had had trouble enlisting a full complement of wardens—many of our volunteers were taking spring holidays and despite all efforts the roster remained three short. Kevin and his friend, and I, were all called to help, very amateurish and very nervous, but delighted to be involved.

The Morning Room came alive to laughter and conversation as Robert greeted the volunteer staff and saw to the allocation of rooms for the afternoon. Having pinned on our badges and collected books of information, the guides dispersed, many commenting on the lovely condition of the house after its spring-clean, and on the displays of blossom and daffodils that brightened the main rooms.

It is part of the room wardens' job to be in place five minutes before the front door opens, to allow time for contents of the room to be checked. Meanwhile Chris was opening up the final strategic doors which are never unlocked until the house is fully manned. By that time the ticket-seller was in place at the front desk and in the Red Corridor the recruiter sat ready to encourage visitors to become members of the National Trust.

As always, the first visitors of the year were waiting in a small queue for the doors to open. In they came, showing membership cards or buying entry tickets, eager to see what Felbrigg looked like after its winter break.

I was relieved to be assigned to the small and not historically complicated Grey Dressing Room. Despite my worries about answering difficult questions, the main attraction in my room proved to be the metal 'boot bath', which always makes visitors smile.


So early in the year we don't expect a flood of people, but our first day is usually gratifyingly busy. Many Trust members live locally and return to visit us time and time again; over the years some have become familiar faces and old friends. Among our first visitors that year were some of our neighbours, tenants from the estate, who remarked on how clean and shining everything looked—though that was before they reached the tea-room and shop area!

Everyone was most understanding about the difficulties we were facing, and interested to see evidence of the renovations and alterations that were still in progress. The afternoon passed swiftly and pleasantly, the guides having their tea-break one at a time before returning to duty, welcoming the visitors with a smile and a greeting, supplying information when asked (if they were able), and all the time keeping a watchful eye on security.

Some added excitement was caused in the front lobby when smoke was seen issuing from a lady's handbag. A pack of book matches was smouldering by spontaneous combustion, but luckily the ticket-seller saw the smoke before the matches actually burst into flames. The lady was quite shaken and everyone was relieved that the danger was averted in time. If her handbag had caught fire while she was in the Hall, the consequences could have been disastrous. Hoping to prevent another such incident, Chris phoned the restaurant advertised by the matches and alerted them to the problem; they were grateful to be told.

At 6 o'clock Robert and Chris relieved the room wardens and closed the main door, after which I helped Chris close up the house in a routine which was to become very familiar to us. Around 6.45 we were back in our flat, tired but well satisfied with our first day.

## Though the Day Be Long . . .

As the season continued, a more regular pattern of work emerged, especially on the days we were open—in our first season that was every day, including weekends, except Mondays and Fridays. In the mornings, Robert was generally in the office attending to accounts and other paperwork, and making and answering phone calls, while Chris was about the house seeing to callers, workmen, cleaners, routine maintenance jobs and whatever else might occur. After lunch, when the Hall opened to visitors, both of them would be on call about the house attending to numerous duties and handling problems as they arose.

Chris's days usually began at 8 a.m., when he started to open the house. From 8.30 to 12.30 the cleaners were busy with their daily routine of dusting and vacuum-cleaning, and twice a week Gill, the lady who does the flowers for the Hall, would come in to replace the displays with fresh blooms.

After the cleaners had gone, Chris would lock up and hope to have an hour in which to wash, change, and eat lunch. This 'hour', frequently truncated because of duties running beyond

12.30, was often interrupted by unexpected callers such as delivery men who had to be attended to.

Whatever happened, half an hour before opening time he had to be down in the main house, raising the blinds to the required level, depending on the brightness of the day, and turning the heaters up for the comfort of the guides. Then he would join Robert in the Morning Room to greet the room wardens as they came on duty.

During the four hours when visitors are about, their needs are paramount and everything revolves around presenting the Hall in the best possible light for them. Mansion staff become practitioners in the art of public relations. Visitors, and staff, must be kept happy in order to maintain a pleasant atmosphere in the house, so administrator and houseman are constantly on the move, keeping themselves available for the various calls which might be made on their expertise.

Any one of the cash points may need change; the supply of guide books at the front desk will occasionally need replenishing; a car driver may park in the wrong spot and have to be asked to move his vehicle; a guide may ask to be relieved for five minutes; a disabled visitor may need showing the 'escape route' which avoids the stairs. . . . And occasionally there will be a real emergency—someone may be taken ill, or the guides' tea-room will be reported bereft of biscuits.

If there are not enough guides on duty, the houseman also stands in as 'tea relief'. Meanwhile a visitor may ask to speak to the administrator to report damage in the woods or gardens, enquire into some obscure aspect of the house's history, or the shooting, or the fishing rights on the lake—and where *is* the lake? And how do you get to the church without going across a field full of cows? (You don't, unless you have a helicopter.) And occasionally, inevitably, someone will want to make a complaint —a situation that must be handled with discretion.

And then there are always the unpredictable occurrences that could never be included in any job description, however detailed: on one occasion when a disabled visitor was disappointed not to see the upper floor, Chris actually carried her up the stairs while her friends managed her wheelchair, and later he saw her safely down again when she had toured the Library and bedrooms. She was delighted by the unexpected extra service. On the other hand, there was the less pleasant and even more urgent occasion when adult human excreta was trodden along the upper floor and two bedrooms had to be closed temporarily while Chris cleaned up the mess.

At the end of the afternoon, while Robert gathered in the day's cash, Chris closed the main door and walked through the show rooms to make sure the house was clear, at the same time relieving the room wardens and thanking them for their help. As he moved through the house he turned off heaters, pulled down blinds, turned on dehumidifiers, and locked strategic doors. The routine is designed to allow late visitors time to complete their tour, leave the restaurant, use the lavatories and finish looking round the shop before leaving the house around the time that the houseman reaches the exit point, though occasionally some will linger in the shop.

When this preliminary walk-through was done and the outer doors all secured, Chris retraced his steps yet again, this time closing shutters, locking more securely, and performing final security checks as he went—the attic stairs; the lavatories; the kitchen areas and corridors. . . . Meanwhile the other staff were completing their own close-down routines and leaving, one by one. When the last of them had gone, the final door could be locked.

Barring last-minute delays, he was generally finished soon after 6.30, by which time he was ready to sit down and rest his aching legs. Those stairs are killers to the thigh muscles and he probably climbed them a dozen times a day, not to mention walking the long corridors, backwards and forwards all afternoon. (One of our friends once lent him a pedometer, which demonstrated that during one typical, not especially busy, afternoon he walked fifteen miles without ever leaving the house!)

Needless to say, very few days are entirely routine. The above is just the basic pattern on to which other demands and duties are grafted as they occur.

Despite the drawbacks of renovation work still going on about her, Joan was determined to have her tea-room fully operational by the first Tuesday in April, so on the previous day—a 'closed' Monday—all hands turned to getting the place ready. Notices were rewritten, chairs and tables moved and the floor cleared of debris left by workmen. Lampshades were taken down, cleaned and replaced, and the display of shining copper utensils, already polished by the cleaners, was dusted again. One of my own contributions was the typing out of the menu.

By Tuesday morning Joan was able to organise her chairs and tables into their pre-planned pattern and at 2 o'clock, when the doors opened on the third day of the season, the tea-room was ready to serve its first cream teas. Visitors expressed their appreciation of the new facilities, the improved servery area and the more spacious seating accommodation. They were, happily, unaware of the chaos continuing behind the scenes.

During hours when visitors were not about, the new servery and kitchen area had to be re-floored. The floor layers, arriving at 9 o'clock one morning, couldn't start their work until a large cupboard had been moved, but they declared that furniture moving was not part of their job; the cupboard had to be shifted before they would begin. The cupboard was too big for Chris to handle on his own, but two builders from the Red Corridor kindly offered a hand, as did an electrician who happened to be working in the Hall. With a great deal of sweat and strain, the four men moved the cupboard.

The floor laying took three days and the layers left dirty marks and scratches on walls and skirting which had been newly decorated, so when they had finished the painter moved in again, after which the big cupboard was manhandled back into place by the same team of kind volunteers.

A day or two later, plumbers fixed new taps in the preparation room and it began to look as though the work in the restaurant was coming to an end. Then at shut-down time Chris discovered that the shutters wouldn't close over the new taps. Since he couldn't leave them open all night he had to turn carpenter and cut neat pieces out of the wood to accommodate the taps. This was one of the nights when he *didn't* get back to the flat by 6.30. Ah, well . . .

Throughout the year, personnel from regional office visit Felbrigg on business: the land agent often has cause to call; someone else may arrive to check on our heaters and their efficiency; the attics and cellars have to be inspected; the fabric of the house is examined frequently and discussions held on how best to maintain it.

One of the decisions arrived at as a result of these visits was that too much light was getting into the Morning Room and the Great Hall, neither of which was suitable to be fitted with the blinds that help to protect other rooms when the sun is bright. It was agreed that scrim curtains should be fitted to the bottom half of the windows, to keep out at least some of the damaging light. The Trust's fabric workshop would make the curtains, but the finer details of how they could be fitted in place was a problem left for Chris to solve.

In between his other duties, he measured up the windows of the Morning Room and the Great Hall. Short curtains had evidently been used in the past, though some of the metal fittings had come loose from ancient and friable stonework and some were lost altogether; new ones must be acquired. However, scouring Norfolk's hardware stores only proved that suitable fittings were no longer available: Chris was obliged to design his own, modelling them on the old ones still in the window mullions, taking pains to get the design exactly right on paper before taking them to the local blacksmith, who agreed to make them.

A week or so later, they were ready. Now came the careful drilling of precious stonework, causing considerable anxiety, and then the fixing of the fittings. In most stages of these operations, I was called upon to supply physical help and moral support; it could have gone wrong, after all. Fortunately, thanks to skill and good planning, it didn't; it all worked fine, and anyone who didn't know better would assume those fittings had always been there.

The original brass curtain rods had been located in a store room where they had been left to go to rust. To complete the job, they needed to be sanded to a smooth finish and burnished so that the curtains would slip on to them.

After a few weeks, when the curtains were delivered from the National Trust fabric workshop at nearby Blickling Hall, they were swiftly hung in place. It was satisfying to see Chris's ingenuity rewarded with success, but in another way it was a sad day: the rooms looked gloomy with half the light shut out, and though we knew it was in a good cause we couldn't help feeling a little dismayed that in order to preserve the place for posterity the Hall was being made that fraction less appealing for present visitors. Our room guides all agreed. However, it was surprising how soon we got used to the curtains and forgot they were there. After a while, regular visitors ceased to remark on them too.

## Free Days

With the house open, Saturdays and Sundays were of course working days, so off-duty time for the administrator and the houseman had to be reorganised, one and a half days a week each. Chris's full day off was to be a Friday, when the house was closed.

'Days off', however, proved to be moveable, or more often dispensable, feasts.

During the first month of our first season, Chris managed only one complete day off. On the first Friday, five different callers were expected—a man to service the steam pressure-boiler in the tea-room; a freezer repairer; a picture expert; a photographer, and the floor layers (this day saw the moving of that huge cupboard, among other things). Robert couldn't possibly have dealt with all of these people alone, so Chris stayed in to help. On the second Friday, work on the shop was almost completed and in order that it should be ready for opening as soon as possible Chris spent all morning sorting the place out, then cleaning and washing down the corridor after the workmen had finished; during his lunch hour two reps called needing his attention—one with catering items, another with cleaning materials—and in the afternoon he went to the blacksmith's to collect the curtain fittings mentioned above, then drove on to a local town to purchase various items for the Hall, later fixing up an electrical cable for the shop.

Time off in lieu is supposed to be taken, but in practice there is seldom an opportunity to catch up with lost free time; there is always far too much to be done.

Realising that Chris had gone a fortnight without a break from work, Robert told him to "take it easy" the following Monday, when we were closed to the public and for once there was not much activity apart from a photographer who would be about the house taking pictures for use on postcards or slides. The man was regularly used by the Trust and should have been capable of working without supervision, but after Chris walked into the Drawing Room just as the photographer caught his tripod on the chandelier (luckily without causing any damage), he felt it necessary to keep a close eye on proceedings.

In the afternoon the photographer decided to take some outside shots, so Chris came up to the flat to relax for a while, but within a short time the doorbell summoned him again. The photographer was back, looking rather pale and distressed. He had failed to notice that the fence of a nearby field was electrified —until he was astride it.

The third weekend of the month was Easter.

## Easter

Easter is one of the busiest times in a National Trust property, the first holiday weekend of the year, when everyone who is not

A somewhat distressed photographer

committed to working tries to get out and visit places, and when old friends of the Hall take the opportunity to call in and see what changes have been made over the winter.

This year the weather was fine, sunny and quite warm. Early on Good Friday, Robert and his wife Eve went off to their cottage for a day or two, leaving Chris and me in charge of the Hall, along with our older son, Andrew, who was home from university.

Though Chris had to be on duty, we hoped that Good Friday would be relatively quiet—the Hall was closed, and cleaners and workmen were taking their bank holiday entitlement. Chris chose to spend his morning doing odd jobs which he hadn't been able to fit in elsewhere, including roping Andrew and me in to help fix up some new notice boards; then we took an alfresco lunch in the Rose Garden. Not having a garden of our own, we seize such opportunities when they present themselves.

The Rose Garden, and the adjoining front courtyard, are protected only by a simple iron fence which separates them from the pasture, across which runs the approach path for the Hall. The weather was glorious, the daffodils a wonderful sight bobbing across the pasture. But the sunshine brought visitors, who evidently expected to find the Hall open on Good Friday. They walked up from the car park, lingering over the notice that states our times and days of opening. Eventually they approached and asked if we were open, though some of them obviously disbelieved the answer. After all *we* were in the garden, were we not?

After several such interruptions to our lunch, we made a strategic withdrawal. There were still a few jobs that Chris wanted to see to, including persuading Andrew to help move some boxes of guide books, for which chore a strong young assistant came in handy.

Easter Saturday morning found the three of us in the Morning Room, rehanging the last of the enormous paintings which belonged there. This lengthy job, calling for great care in its execution, had been left over from when the Morning Room was stripped for dry rot treatment. It had now become a priority because a concert was due to be held in the Morning Room at the beginning of May. The grand piano, too, had to be moved to a better spot, with consequent rearrangement of other furniture and lifting and relaying of carpets.

Before lunch our younger son Kevin arrived, briefly home from his nursing training in Norwich, and Robert returned in time for opening. The normal 'open day' routine took up the afternoon, but closing down was a family affair, with the boys and me all doing our share of shutter-closing. In the evening Chris was busy in the office, totting up the day's cash, since Robert had a social engagement that evening. He finished work at 10 p.m.

On Easter Day, being short of room wardens that afternoon, Chris asked Kevin and me to stand in again. Nor was Andrew left out for long: the excellent weather brought a great many visitors to the house, the unexpected rush causing strain on the tea-room staff. Being the only one of the family still available, Andrew answered the manageress's plea for extra help clearing tables and washing up.

On Easter Monday, even more visitors crowded the Hall, on a day which highlighted the problems of the layout of the house, whose architects had never envisaged a daily influx of hundreds of visitors. During the afternoon a member asked to see the administrator and complained about people entering our gardens illicitly by means of a 'No Entry' gate near the car park. Unfortunately, short of employing someone to stand outside and watch this vulnerable gate, which is not visible from the house, there was no immediate solution to this continuing problem. Robert could only thank the man for his observation and say we would do what we could.

Another problem of ingress was demonstrated when other visitors, coming only to the shop and tea-room by a side entrance, gained access to the staircase and upstairs rooms of the Hall via the route to the lavatories, without passing the front desk. Such people, coming from the wrong direction and interrupting the flow, were breaking the rules—not to mention the fire regulations —and causing upset among both visitors and guides, who reported their concern as Robert and Chris made their regular patrols through the house.

Unless they caught people coming through the wrong door, there was little they could do. The answer would be to build other lavatories, away from the main visitor route, but for that money, space and time would have to be found at some future date. For the moment, we all had to keep watch and try to stop infiltrators, out of fairness to members and other visitors who *had* paid their entry fee and come in the correct way. We solved the problem eventually by having an extra guide on duty in the relevant spot, directing traffic.

Evening events—mainly musical concerts—had been planned to take place roughly once a month throughout the season. These events were to be held in the Morning Room, which can accommodate an audience of sixty, on Friday evenings, with an optional candle-lit supper after the performance. The first concert—a recital by a well-known pianist—was to be held in early May.

Various activities in connection with the concert had been going on at intervals for weeks: Robert had been to court to obtain the necessary licence; the pianist had called to assess the piano—a Bechstein grand—and, since he was not very happy with its condition, his misgivings had been reported to regional office who had sent an expert in to take a look; woodworm was diagnosed, and though it was probably not active the required treatment was applied.

During the week, seventy new concert chairs were delivered to the back door—at 11 o'clock in the morning on an "open" day. They had to be carted to the Morning Room, out of the way, before afternoon visitors started arriving. I offered to help. Chris could manage four chairs at a time; I contented myself with two. The job got done.

My parents had arrived to spend a few days with us, the first opportunity they had had to view our new situation. My father in particular was almost envious; he said it was just the sort of job he would have liked, given the chance when he was younger.

## Mirrors to an Exhibition

Although the Friday of the concert should have been our day off, Chris was busier than ever, not only with preparations for the evening. In the morning, certain items from the house were to be collected by a van sent by the Victoria and Albert Museum, which was borrowing them for an exhibition of Rococo furniture. Felbrigg boasts particularly fine examples of this style, especially a pair of pier glasses, an overmantel mirror, a pier table and a pair of gilt wall brackets.

Although we were flattered that the V & A should ask to borrow these pieces we were also concerned for their welfare. The pier table had already been decreed too delicate to move from its place and the two mirrors which would be leaving us were most vulnerable, having ornate and fragile wood and gesso frames.

However, experts had prepared special crates. When the fronts had been removed the mirrors were firmly attached to the backs of the crates; then the fronts were replaced, the tops were taken off and tiny polystyrene beads poured in to fill every space. It had been stipulated by the Trust that the mirrors must travel upright at all times to avoid stress.

Despite all this planning, when the museum's van arrived on Friday morning to transport the pieces, it was not tall enough to allow the eighteenth-century pier glass to stand upright. Our regional historic buildings representative had to be consulted; after a deal of agonising, he agreed that the pier glass could be packed into the van at a slightly backward angle, but still as upright as possible: if the frame broke, or the glass shattered, the mirror was irreplaceable. Eventually, all the items were safely packed and signed into the care of the museum's specialist transporters.

The absence of the overmantel mirror from its place in the Red Bedroom provided a special talking point: the wallpaper in this room, dating from c.1840, had appeared to be a tasteful pattern of broad stripes in grey and crimson; the removal of the mirror revealed the truth—that originally the paper was a startling scarlet and pinky-lilac, with gilding on the borders of the stripes. These colours blazed out, mirror-shaped, above the fireplace, contrasting with the faded glory of the rest of the wall and reminding us that in their hey-day these old houses were a riot of colour.

## A Concert Evening

Having seen the exhibition items on their way, Chris turned his full attention to the concert that evening. He moved the smaller pieces of furniture which normally reside in the Morning Room and stored them in the staircase hall. During the afternoon the piano tuner arrived as promised and while he was exercising his skill Chris arranged the concert chairs in rows to comply with fire regulations, and checked that emergency lights were working. Brass candlesticks were taken out of store and polished, and fresh candles fixed for use during the candle-lit supper, whose preparation began when Joan and her team arrived late in the afternoon.

By 6 o'clock at the latest, Chris planned to be in the flat, having a bath and getting changed, ready to be at the door by 6.30 when the first concert-goers would appear. Robert had asked me to help, too, so I was busy putting on my own glad-rags in between preparing a meal for four. My parents were agog at all the unusual activity.

During the afternoon, a slight complication arose. The mansion was contracted to provide a place in which the concert performer might rest and prepare for the evening. Usually the administrator would lend a room of his larger flat for this purpose. However, that day Eve found it impossible to get home from her work before 6.15, at which time Robert had to collect her from the railway station, so he asked that on this occasion *we* might supply a room for the pianist's use. In our small flat the only place available was our spare bedroom, which my parents were using; but they agreed to vacate it for the evening and hurried to stow their belongings out of sight.

When the pianist had finished his afternoon rehearsal, he and his companion—charming gentlemen both, and most grateful for the trouble we had taken—came up to the flat. It was then almost 6.30. The pianist confided that he liked to lie down for at least half an hour before a performance, then slowly and quietly get ready.

"But . . ." said Chris, perplexed, "the concert's due to start in half an hour."

"Oh, no," replied the pianist, "it doesn't start until 7.30. That's what I was told."

Whoever gave him this information was mistaken—tickets, and posters, all proclaimed that the concert would begin at 7 p.m. sharp. It was one of those unfortunate mix-ups that do sometimes occur and we were relieved that the pianist was such a pleasant man, not given to outbursts of artistic temperament: he agreed to be ready as soon as possible after 7, if we could somehow keep the audience amused until he appeared.

But there was no time for lengthy discussion. The audience would be arriving any minute and Chris and I were both expected to be down at the front desk in time to greet the first arrivals. My parents stayed watching television in the sitting room, hardly daring to move in case they disturbed the pianist's concentration.

At 6.30 prompt, Chris and I opened the front door and the first concert-goers appeared, offering their tickets. Also on duty were two of our room wardens, to keep a general eye on security and help to direct people through rooms and around hallways and corridors, to order their interval drinks and to find the cloakrooms.

There is always a good deal of information to impart to a concert audience as it gathers: seats are not numbered, so it's a good idea to reserve a chair, with a coat or scarf, before going to order drinks. Yes, soft drinks and coffee are readily available if preferred. Some of the concert-goers have sent money for tickets which are held at the door, others have booked tickets and will pay when they arrive; it's my job to sort them out. Occasionally people turn up expecting to be able to purchase a ticket at the door but, with a maximum of sixty seats available, our concerts are usually sold out; so late-comers will be disappointed. Programmes are distributed, queries answered, and we watch out for high heels, which are banned because of our wooden floors and precious carpets.

A warning about the wearing of sharp, pointed heels, besides being displayed at the entrance, is printed on the tickets, but some ladies fail to notice it; they have come out dressed up, looking glamorous; some are not pleased to be asked to exchange their elegant shoes for disposable blue plastic 'slippers' that look like shower caps, though some will comply and treat it as a joke. Some prefer to go in stockinged feet, others promise to walk on tiptoe; an occasional one may be offended by our request and refuse to do anything about it—"It's hard luck; I'm not taking *my* shoes off!"

Between us, Chris and I juggled these various problems as fifty-eight people filtered in and mingled about the corridors, taking the opportunity to look round the Great Hall under the watchful eye of our two helpers. As 7 o'clock approached, they all began to drift towards their seats in the concert room.

Robert appeared, freshly garbed in his best suit and anxious to know how things were going. Told of the mistake over timing, he decided to delay his opening announcements for a few minutes. We waited. The Morning Room was full of buzzing, expectant people, only two seats remaining empty. Those two spaces were far apart—it always happens—and we could only hope that the missing couple would not mind sitting distant from each other. At least their late arrival meant we had a legitimate reason for delaying the start.

A car swept into the gravel courtyard and parked, the final pair of concert-goers hurrying in, all apologies for their lateness. Their consternation at the separateness of the available seats was swiftly dispersed when the rest of the audience kindly made adjustments and two adjacent vacant chairs appeared as if by magic. The audience was gathered. What of the artiste?

Chris dashed back to our flat, some distance away, and returned breathless to report that the pianist would be down in five minutes. It was up to Robert to fill the gap. We could delay no longer. The audience was becoming restive.

Robert stepped into the Morning Room to make his announcements—about future concerts, about the suppers, and any other message that might be useful and informative. He filled in with a good deal of affable waffling, keeping the audience amused and bemused—some of them were looking at their watches, glancing at the door, obviously wondering at the prolonged delay. Robert too started to look anxious, hoping for a sign that he could end his diatribe.

At last the pianist appeared in a doorway. A signal to the administrator let him round off his chat with an introduction. The pianist walked in amid a burst of applause. . . .

The concert began. Behind the scenes, sighs of relief were breathed all round as music floated along the hallways. The audience was rapt. While the concert continued, we went about our duties on tip-toe.

Having cashed up and made a note of moneys taken, I handed

78

the accounts over to Robert, who stood guard while Chris and I grabbed a quick meal with my parents in the flat. Having eaten, we returned to help with the security watch, and in the interval we directed people to the bar, answered questions about the house and generally tried to make visitors feel welcome. It being a mild evening, the Rose Garden door was opened and people drifted out with their wine to enjoy the air—except for those who used the opportunity to light up cigarettes on which they puffed fervently before entering the 'No Smoking' zone again as the interval ended.

During the second half of the concert, Chris turned on lamps which he had earlier placed in the front rooms of the house, upstairs and down. It would be dark when everyone left and the Hall looks wonderful when its windows are lit from inside; it seems to come alive and exude an aura of older, more elegant times, just a little touch which we hope will add to the enjoyment of the evening for our visitors.

The concert ended with an encore shortly after 9 o'clock and people began to emerge from the Morning Room, some to take their leave of us, others making for the restaurant. Most of them expressed their delight in the pianist's performance. Our helpers —a husband and wife team from our pool of volunteers— also departed with our thanks for their invaluable presence. Meanwhile, the diners, including Robert and Eve, took their places at candle-lit supper tables in the Old Kitchen restaurant.

With the Hall quiet for the time being, Chris and I began to rearrange the Morning Room, stacking the concert chairs so that the carpet could be rolled back and the piano returned to its usual place; then the chairs were packed into a bay, covered with a dust sheet, and the other furniture brought back—tables, chairs, a tea-poy, a firescreen. . . . By the time the first of the diners had finished their meal and returned to the front door, the Morning Room was transformed back into its familiar, elegant self.

Now we could relax, and ourselves enjoy a glass of wine while we stood by to see the last of the visitors out. The night being dark, we offered a little assistance by torchlight through our unlit porch, but once into the courtyard the lights from the Hall guided the way.

On such occasions the old house glows with light from all its front windows, and when the sky is clear the moon may be shining and the stars will be out in full force—here at Felbrigg they are not dimmed by town lights. Sharing our visitors' enjoyment as they leave, we really appreciate our fortune in living in such a place.

When the last diner had gone, we started our locking-up routine, switching out lights: the close-down procedure was the same as every day. All that remained was to share the last few minutes, feeling satisfaction in a successful evening, as Joan and her staff tidied up their domain and departed to their homes. Finally, Chris turned a last key and we climbed wearily up the stairs to our own home. It was 11.45 p.m.

And it didn't really end there; with no cleaners on duty on a Saturday, in the morning the lavatories needed cleaning and the kitchen floors had to be washed before Chris could start on his usual list of duties.

After a few more concerts we had the routine perfected, each of us knowing what to do, and when. Such days mean long hours and a great deal of hard work for both house and restaurant staff, but our efforts are rewarded by the pleasure the evenings afford our visitors. We want them to regard 'our' house as a warm, friendly place to which they will want to return many times, and to our delight a good few of them do come back, to almost every concert, some regularly driving fifty miles or more to spend an evening at Felbrigg Hall.

## Odds and Ends

The season continued with the regular pattern of open days, with visitors about during the afternoons and at other times delivery men calling, goods to be stacked and stored, running repairs to be seen to and staff problems to settle. Small essential jobs cropped up from day to day as they will in every household; it's just that in a National Trust property the possibilities are magnified in proportion to the size of the place and the number of people involved. When dealing with the public almost anything can happen. Staff must be able to cope with any eventuality.

There was, for instance, the baby left sleeping near the ticket desk. . . .

Babies' pushchairs must be left in the lobby: they take up a great deal of space, are too low down to be easily visible in a crowd and may therefore be a hazard to other visitors, especially the elderly, not to mention possible danger to the child if someone falls on him. Usually, of course, the pushchairs left behind are empty.

This particular baby was angelic, sleeping soundly; it would have been a shame to disturb him—"He always sleeps like a top in the afternoons, he'll be out like that for an hour or two," the mother assured our obliging ticket-seller, who agreed that she would keep an eye on the infant; she loves children and is herself a doting grandmother. Of course, no sooner were the parents out of earshot than the child began to wail. Its cries penetrated the lobby, Great Hall and beyond, despite all the ticket-seller's grand-maternal skills.

Summoned by the unaccustomed noise, Chris appeared. He took charge of the infant, removed it from its pushchair and soon quietened it, had it cooing and smiling contentedly. When he returned it to its conveyance the little angel seemed on the point of sleep again.

But as soon as he departed the child woke and wailed afresh. In between greeting visitors, and dispensing tickets and guide books, the lady on the desk renewed her efforts to pacify the baby, but when *she* picked it up it was sick all down her. She will never forget it.

On another occasion, two other infants were the innocent cause of a less amusing problem:

Chris was on his usual afternoon 'walkabout' through the house on a busy day when he heard a room warden's voice raised in alarm and protest, exclaiming, "You can't do that here!" Chris hurried to her aid and discovered a young mother seated on the windowseat in the Yellow Bedroom, preparing to breastfeed her baby in full view of other visitors. Only feet away, yet another young woman with a baby slung behind her was unpacking a clean nappy, wipes and talcum powder, bent on changing her infant on the other windowseat. Both of them were stubbornly ignoring the room warden's admonishments.

Informed that a chair for nursing purposes was provided in the ladies' cloakroom, the first young woman replied that she was not going to feed *her* baby in a public toilet; the child was hungry and she would feed it where she chose; likewise her friend was entitled to change her baby—it was their right to do so.

Aware of the room warden's distress, and of the embarrassment felt by passing visitors, Chris insisted that the feeding and changing could not take place in the bedroom; the young women must follow him to a more private spot. He took them to a quiet corner where there was more room, less traffic, and where they were shielded from immediate gaze, so the incident ended without undue unpleasantness. Just another of those unexpected moments that add spice to a busy day.

Most children, sleeping or waking, are a delight and we love to see them. And we are grateful to parents who keep their offspring under control and do not let them swing on the ropes, scatter the stanchions or leap on the beds.

We have a special young person's guide for sale at the desk, with things to do and look for and puzzles to fill in—we are pleased to notice that ninety-nine per cent of the pencils lent out by our ticketsellers for this purpose are politely returned later, with smiles and thanks. Our room wardens, too, generally have something of interest to point out to children in every room. When youngsters' curiosity is aroused they ask some penetrating questions that confound even the most erudite among our staff.

## Flowers

As an extra touch for visitors' enjoyment, we keep flowers in nearly every show room of the Hall—three large displays downstairs, three smaller posies for the bedrooms. They are changed at least twice a week, and usually looked after by Gill, one of the tenants living off the courtyard behind the Hall, with the help of her husband, Henry. The flowers mean a lot of work and entail much responsibility, all of it undertaken on a purely voluntary basis.

For most of the year our own gardens supply the raw material, though on occasion it may be augmented by blooms from Gill's garden—one of only three private garden areas behind the stable block—or from one of her friends'. She selects whatever is in season, together with foliage to enhance the display; then she and her husband visit the various rooms of the Hall to remove the fading flowers and take them to their own kitchen, where they are discarded and the new ones arranged. This can be a lengthy, and messy, process. It takes most of a morning, twice a week.

Her brief is not to create an artistic masterpiece but simply to enhance the room, as if the lady of the house had stepped into the garden to pick some flowers and casually put them in a vase. Even so, creating this 'casual' effect takes great skill: the décor in the rooms has to be considered; and some displays will be seen from varying angles while others will show visitors only one face.

Having created glorious fresh arrangements, Gill carefully carries each display all the way from her own home, through the Hall's corridors and rooms, with Henry following behind with a watering can to top up the container and a cloth to mop up any drops, so as not to mark the polish of fine tables. Back and forth they go. We are extremely grateful for their efforts, for the skill that brings so much pleasure and so many compliments, and for their patience in putting up with the mess in their kitchen.

With the season well into its stride, a shortage of room wardens at weekends became apparent; I was requested to stand in on a regular basis until this deficiency could be filled.

We keep a waiting list of interested people, but they must be prepared to commit their time on a regular basis over the season; an occasional day as and when it fits into their own social round is not of much use to us. But we can't just summon up new guides at a moment's notice; they have to be interviewed first before they decide if the job is what they expected, and then they have to work out what days they can spare. It all takes time.

However, I was pleased to be involved; it made me feel that I was an integral part of the house and its doings, not simply a convenient pair of extra hands. It also gave me an opportunity to get to know the room wardens, and the house, better, and by helping out I was also relieving the pressures on Chris and Robert. All the same, I have to admit that after six months at Felbrigg I was beginning to hope that soon the pressure on *me* would ease and I might have the chance to concentrate on my own work.

Nor was I alone: Eve was also put to use when needed, though on less frequent occasions since she was not available very often. Even so, she still helped her own husband with paperwork, and arranged flowers when Gill was away.

As the months went by it was becoming apparent to me that being a National Trust wife, resident on a property, is by definition to be involved in the work. It is all around you, twenty-four hours of the day. To remain aloof would take someone of iron will and stubborn resolve. You're there, on the spot all the time, readily available in any emergency. If no one else answers a doorbell or a phone, *you* do. Staff come to you with problems, queries and comments that they hope will get passed on; room wardens use you as a messenger service; your husband takes for granted that you will help out in any one of a dozen capacities at a moment's notice. And, most of the time, out of loyalty to him, you do. And, most of the time, you don't mind at all.

Only occasionally do you wonder whatever happened to the private life you once had.

## Room Wardens

Visitors frequently ask how the rooms are allocated among our volunteers. Do they always attend in the same room? Are they told which room they will stand in? Do they take each room in turn? The answer is that every property has its own method, evolved over the years.

At Felbrigg, a lottery system has proved most acceptable to everyone concerned. Every other system seemed to bring mutterings about favouritism and complaints from some volunteers who felt aggrieved at never getting the more desirable rooms—though which room is desirable and which is not is a matter of personal preference.

The lottery works by means of draughts on a board. Names of the various rooms have been painted on the draughts and when all the wardens are gathered each day the draughts are arranged, name-side down, and shuffled, finally being laid in a circle on the board. Each volunteer picks a draught and reads what fortune has brought that day.

There are cries of, "Oh, good, my favourite room!" or, "Not Tea Relief again!"—"I'll have that," offers a gentleman who enjoys the peripatetic assignment. Another experienced guide, who loves best the big state rooms and hates being stuck upstairs, murmurs drily: "I *might* be persuaded to relinquish the Chinese Bedroom." Someone will probably swap with him. If not, he'll do the Chinese Bedroom without further demur. But some people prefer being in the bedrooms; they find the main state rooms rather daunting. The swapping, or not, is all part of the fun.

Most times the system works and all are happy, though occasionally someone may end up with a room he or she dislikes. But they all take it in good part because it's only for one afternoon. Over the season everyone has a fair chance to be in preferred rooms.

But a room warden's job is not all light-hearted. The serious side is the security aspect, and the need to ensure that no damage occurs. A good measure of tact is called for. Some visitors object to being asked to put out cigarettes, remove shoes with pointed heels, take off rucksacks and leave them behind, keep children under control, and *not to touch*. However politely they are reminded, still some of them will take offence, though there is always a very good reason for the rules which the Trust lays down.

Despite all the 'Please do not touch' notices, certain visitors insist on fingering fabrics or picking up the porcelain "to see who made it". Their impulse is quite innocent, and understandable; we sympathise, but one slip of their fingers and a curtain fabric, paper-thin with age, is torn, or a precious plate could be gone for ever. Certain items are more fragile than they look; others may have been mended only recently. Our volunteers are there to guard against accidental damage of this kind.

But however many notices we put out, some people don't see them. One classic case involved some delicate chairs dating from the time of William and Mary. We have only three of these chairs left and the canework on them is particularly fine and fragile. In order to display them and yet protect them, we keep them under the stairs where they are not easily accessible, and on one of them stands a notice saying 'Please do not sit on these chairs'. Nevertheless, one afternoon, Chris on his rounds discovered a lady taking her ease in this spot.

He paused, hardly believing his eyes, saying, "Excuse me. Did you see the notice asking you not to sit on the chairs?"

"Oh, yes," replied the lady with a bright smile, nodding at the chair beside her. "It's all right—I moved it."

## Outside Events

On summer Sundays we often have events taking place outside. During our first year, in May alone, we had folk dancers performing on one afternoon and on another a Rolls-Royce rally, when vehicles old and new were brought up and displayed in the courtyard, paint gleaming and chrome mirroring Jacobean bays. These and similar events added interest to an afternoon out for our visitors.

Other 'outside events' concerned the lake; frogs and toads; and the breeding herd of Red Devon cattle.

A vigilant neighbour called the police to two poachers fishing

Taking her ease where she shouldn't be

out of season on the lake; the men were later prosecuted and fined. Someone else reported a rash of dead frogs lying by the lakeside; the water board was called in to investigate, but since nothing sinister was found we assumed the deaths to be a result of over-breeding. As if to confirm this, coming home late one rainy night we stopped when our headlights descried the road apparently alive, covered in jumping stones. Curious, we both climbed out of the car, only to find ourselves walking on tiny frogs. The roadway was covered in them, thousand upon thousand of them, all hopping up from their spawning grounds around the lake and heading . . . where?—to the woods? Unable to wait all night until the mass migration ended, we eventually drove on, feeling like murderers as the minute creatures were squashed under our wheels.

Perhaps some of the 'frogs' were toads; these creatures live and breed beneath the gratings outside our cellars. The trouble is, visitors see them and think they are trapped; trapped toads in our gratings are frequently reported by distressed persons, both children and adults. After a rash of such complaints, Chris and I spent an evening clearing out the gratings and trying to chase the toads away from their 'captivity', with the result that in the morning the toads were all back down where they belonged. We concluded that they must like it there; they probably think that their warty god lives up above the gratings, dropping down tasty insects in the cool of the night.

As for the cows and their calves, they provide much interest. The young calves are a delight to watch, though on the inevitable day when they are separated from their mothers and put into a smaller field, prior to going to market, we can hear them calling mournfully to each other all night.

When calves are born out in the fields, as they frequently are during spring and summer, visitors will rush to the Hall to report the event; perhaps they think we should call a midwife. But since there are occasions when a cow is in real trouble Chris always checks these reports if he can, and makes sure the calf is all right. If he has any doubts, he calls the farmer. He has been attacked by cows protecting their new-born offspring, and had to run for it, but on several occasions he has been able to alert the farmer and save the life of a cow and/or her calf.

And then there are the bulls, necessary in a breeding herd. Despite the warning notices, some people are annoyed to find a bull in a field across which they must walk to the church or the lake. They refuse to believe that the bulls are far less hostile than the cows—get between a new mother and her calf and watch out! Even the farmer and his men have been seen taking to their heels, heading for the safety of the nearest tree to escape the charge of an angry cow.

Late one afternoon, as Chris was closing the gates, he fell into conversation with a group of teenage cyclists lingering in the park.

"Is that a bull in that field with those cows?" one youth asked. "What's it doing there?"

"Well . . ." How to put it delicately? "It's a stock herd. The cows aren't used for milking, they're used for producing calves."

"Yes, I can see that," said the cyclist. "But what do they want the bull for? What does it do?"

All kinds of answers crossed the mind. *They could hardly use a budgerigar*, for instance. "What do bulls usually do? It breeds. Actually the farmer goes in with it every morning and shows it what to do."

The youth and his friends fell about laughing at that. They were, after all, children of the 1980s and well acquainted with the facts of life. "No, really! I mean, they don't really need bulls any more, do they? They do it by artificial insemination. I saw it on a programme on TV."

He was astounded, and delighted, when informed that such new-fangled methods aren't in use everywhere, and here at Felbrigg good old Mother Nature still appears to work pretty well.

We always thought that talk about city children believing milk to be manufactured in bottles was exaggerated. Maybe not.

## Visitors Various

We certainly have an assortment of people coming to the Hall, all ages, from all walks of life. Princes, peers, priests and proletariat, all of them extraordinary in their way and all with different interests. Some admire the paintings; some are fascinated by furniture; one may be an expert on clocks; another finds our fire grates of special interest—he worked in the iron industry at one time. We are constantly amazed by the knowledge some of our visitors display.

Others come to soak up the atmosphere, to find out about the history of the people who lived here, to wander in the peace of our gardens, or simply to have a rest. Seeing a group of Hell's Angels approaching, complete with black leather gear, chained and studded, Robert alerted Chris to the possibility of trouble. Chris went to meet the group, chatted with them and discovered that the 'Angels' had come just to have a cup of tea. They were quieter and more polite than certain expensively-dressed visitors we have known.

On another day, Chris found himself being quizzed about the house by an attractive American lady. Americans seem to be especially interested in old houses and this one was no exception, a charming lady who before she left introduced herself and shook him by the hand, thanking him for his time. Her name meant nothing to him. Only later, watching television, did he realise that one of Wogan's glamorous guests was that same American lady—a well-known actress. She was just one of the famous faces we see from time to time, some of them regular visitors.

Yet another type of visitor was exemplified by the lady in a wheelchair—physically disabled, blind and deaf, she was being taken round by a friend with whom she was able to communicate only by touch of fingers on palm in sign language. Intrigued, Chris asked the helper what her friend could possibly gain from a visit to a house such as ours if she could neither see nor hear. The helper put the question, signing words on the disabled lady's hand, and translated the reply: "She can sense the atmosphere, and feel the space about her." Told that the "man in charge" was asking, the lady wanted to touch and "see" him; she felt his hands and then his face. She had, she conveyed through her companion, enjoyed her visit very much. This meeting was a humbling, moving experience that Chris will never forget.

Naturally we do not entirely satisfy everyone, not all the time. While the majority love the intimate, homely atmosphere, some would prefer to see explanatory labels on everything; others complain that it's already "just like a museum". Some find

Felbrigg not grand enough for their taste; some are daunted by its grandeur. And some have individual views for which there is no answer. One lady, seen striding rapidly through the bedrooms heading for the exit less than two minutes after we opened, could hardly articulate her distress at the colour of the guide book cover, which is purple. She couldn't wait to get out of the house and away from that awful colour.

## Base Campers

Towards the end of May, the base camp was again in use for a week, this time by a group of art students who were staying in the accommodation and using the Hall and its environs as subjects for their talent. They arrived late on a Friday night and rang the bell, summoning Chris from the flat. He went down to show them the facilities and explain the rules and regulations which they must obey for their own comfort and safety and that of other tenants, staff and visitors. He checked the inventory with their leader, and agreed the reading on the electricity meter. He also explained that they must—please—not park their cars in the stable yard, where they might block garages and reserved parking spaces. Phone messages from friends or relatives would be passed on only in case of real emergency; the milkman came on such and such days; the refuse bins were in this shed—and so forth.

Most base campers are well behaved and welcome. Some can be more of a problem. This particular group proved to be a little of both. In the few days they were here they sat dotted about the pasture and gardens wielding paintbrushes; some of them started at sunrise, presumably to catch the early morning light on the Hall. We saw one girl dancing dreamily on the pasture in bare feet at dawn, 'dabbling in the dew' like the milkmaids in the song.

One of the young men drank a whole bottle of whisky and 'went berserk', though we heard about that only after the event from tenants who were disturbed. The students also insisted on leaving their cars in the yard, causing aggravation to members of staff whose spaces were taken. And, when they left, there was paint smeared all over the base camp floor and a distinct scent of smoke from unusual substances about which we tried not to speculate. Perhaps it was joss sticks.

Still, it could have been worse, as more experienced Felbriggians kept telling us: "Just you wait until the Germans come!"

A party of young people from Germany had booked the base camp for three weeks in July. Regaled by tales of their exploits in previous years, we anticipated their arrival with mixed emotions.

# 4

# Summer—The High Holiday Season

### Changes

Azaleas, and rhododendrons in wonderful variety, came into glorious flower in the gardens, while the trees burgeoned towards full rich leaf. The weather continued damp and grey but occasional bursts of sunlight made us feel that summer might not be far away.

Since Fridays were proving difficult to keep free for us to have a day off, Robert suggested that we should take Mondays instead. This too was a 'closed' day and not complicated by monthly concerts, so if Mondays could be kept fairly clear of work we should be able to have some time to ourselves. The arrangement worked pretty well; at least Chris and I could get out and about together again on one day in the week. A slight drawback proved to be that finding lunch, or even a cup of coffee, on a Monday was not easy—in Norfolk, most places have their own time off on that day.

With the improved restaurant facilities providing teas and a wide range of home-made cakes, Joan launched the next stage of her operation and offered lunches, too. The restaurant, and the shop, would open at noon from now on.

This meant reorganising routines; if the restaurant was to be open at 12 o'clock, cloakrooms too must be available and since they were deep in the main house, which was not open until 2 o'clock, certain strategic doors had to be locked during the interim to prevent casual, unsupervised access. A complication would be that the cleaners were still working in the house until 12.30. However, the ladies accepted a slight change in their own pattern of work and a little planning evolved a lunchtime close-down procedure which allowed them a free run and yet did not leave the house vulnerable to straying visitors. Performing this security routine nibbled away another few minutes of Chris's lunch hour, but it was worth it when very soon people were flocking in to sample our lunchtime fare.

## School Tours

In common with most other National Trust mansions, Felbrigg provides special guided tours for schools, and also for other groups seeking a more in-depth study of the house. These tours take place in the morning, when we are closed to the general public, and must be arranged well in advance. Large school parties are usually split into two groups, smaller groups being more manageable. One of our senior room wardens, a former school master who enjoys sharing his knowledge of the house, especially with children, frequently takes one of the groups; Chris takes the other. Each has his own method of imparting information. Both have enough skill to keep the children enthralled.

Usually Chris holds his group back for a few minutes, to allow the others time to get a room or so ahead. If the weather allows, he often keeps them outside, showing them the startling difference between the architecture of the main Jacobean front and the west wing. The front is obviously very old, with leaded windows and stone quoins, its brickwork patched with plaster rendering that is sadly worn and broken by time; in contrast, the west wing is of red brick with tall sash windows. In fact, the Jacobean front predates the west wing by a mere sixty years or so.

Equally startling is the evidence that over the centuries the décor of the Jacobean front has changed dramatically. It was not always mellow and charmingly care-worn as we have grown used to seeing it. Once the brickwork, and the pointing, was painted a bold red; then it was painted white, and finally ochre, before the rendering was applied and scored to give an appearance of stone. The fact that it was never originally intended to be covered in plaster is one reason why the rendering is now breaking away and exposing the rosy brick. Evidence of all these changes still remains to be seen in traces of the different colours of wash in places on the wall.

Another point of interest is the stone lettering blazoned on the bays at the front of the roof. The words read, GLORIA DEO IN EXCELSIS—glory to God in the highest. Latin scholars may point out that the order of the quotation is not correct; strictly speaking, it should be GLORIA IN EXCELSIS DEO, but the stonemason had to fit the words into three bays of equal size, so GLORIA—DEO IN—EXCELSIS was more manageable.

The Windhams who lived here were, in the main, God-fearing, law-abiding people, good squires to their tenants and worthy protectors of the land. The family history holds no horror stories, no priest holes, no secret passage-ways and tales of high romance and derring-do; no, Felbrigg's story holds more subtle attractions, stories of ordinary human triumph and tragedy, humour and sadness, and even a case of notoriety, ending in pitiful loneliness.

Chris will probably allude to some of this during his preliminary talk, providing an intriguing prelude to the school tour.

When the first group has had time to move on, he introduces his party to the Great Hall and so they progress through the house. The history of the building and its occupants is a subject which fascinates him and he is able to transmit his enthusiasm to his young listeners, lacing the lesson with humour and the kind of details that children love—hidden doors, minor scandals, and any hint of ghosts! Questions pour forth from the children; if their guide doesn't keep an eye on the time he will over-run. He could talk for hours about a place he has come to love.

A school party which had booked one of these special tours arrived on a cold, wet morning in June. They planned to spend the day with us, first touring the Hall, then having a picnic lunch and walking in the park and woods during the afternoon.

When the tour ended it was still raining heavily. With resignation, since their coach had driven off and would not be back until 4 o'clock, the teachers decided they would have to eat their lunch under whatever shelter they could find in the picnic area. Since this seemed an uncomfortable way for the children to spend the next couple of hours, Chris suggested they might use the games room of the base camp, off the stable yard. The base camp was not being used at the time and it was certainly a more congenial venue than the woods. The school party departed gratefully, leaving him to do his lunchtime lock-down.

Despite the awful weather—or perhaps because of it—the Hall was busy. Visitors poured in, leaving wet macs, umbrellas and bulky bags in the care of the ticket-seller. Bad weather often brings people to us: holidaymakers want something to do and if they can't sit on the beach or be out in the countryside they may choose to visit a stately home. At least here they are in the dry, they can wander and stare and marvel, read their guide book, chat with the room wardens, and look forward to a hot cup of tea and a piece of home-made cake, followed perhaps by a visit to the shop. On such days the tea-room gets crowded, the windows misted with condensation; people are reluctant to face the inclement weather.

In the midst of a day like this, the school party came straggling back to the front courtyard, poor little mites with miserable faces, draped in dripping raincoats, their hair soaked, their feet wet. Their teacher left them outside and came to ask for help. She had to find something for them all to do for two hours before their coach returned to pick them up. Could Chris suggest anything?

He invited them back in and took them to the lobby, where they divested themselves of their wet things, and then into the Morning Room where they sat on the carpet while he used his ingenuity to amuse them.

## The Morning Room—and 'Mad' Windham

The Morning Room is not usually available to visitors except by prior arrangement. This is because it is set apart from the regular route through the house and also because we use it as a functional room, where meetings are held, where the guides gather of an afternoon, and where our concerts take place. Also, we now keep our concert chairs here, stacked under dust sheets. It would be impractical to have the room open on a regular basis.

However, the Morning Room does contain some interesting pictures and furniture. One particular portrait is of a sweet-faced little boy, aged about six, wearing a blue, skirted jacket. The boy is William Frederick Windham, known to his family as 'Gla' and more notorious later as 'Mad' Windham. He was certainly eccentric, and evidently not very bright: as a young man he fell among bad company and married a fortune-huntress of the *demi-monde*; he was frittering away his fortune, much to the alarm of his uncle and guardian, General Windham. But during a famous court case in 1861 he was judged to be sane, if a spendthrift and fool.

Less than two years later, he had bankrupted the estate. Felbrigg passed out of Windham hands.

Deserted by his wife, William Frederick spent the next few years driving a mail coach between Cromer and Norwich—driving it wildly, much to the consternation of the locals, though he was an expert whip. This may well have been the happiest period of his brief life, among the rough 'common' folk.

His end has a haunting sadness about it. A local paper reported: *'It will be enough for us to draw the curtain with William Frederick Windham's death in the February of 1866 in the little bedroom at the hotel up the leaded staircase past the bar. It was said that in the last few weeks the man who had squandered thousands had not the wherewithal to buy a meal, and when the end had come there was no one to order a coffin for him and a shirt of dead Dan Durrant's had to be put upon him in default of his own.'*

He was twenty-five years old. Poor Gla.

However, despite the profligacy of "Mad" Windham, Felbrigg itself was saved by its next owner, John Ketton, a merchant from Norwich. He bought the estate, the Hall and everything in it and the wonder is that he changed very little. He didn't even move the Windham ancestral portraits from their places in the main rooms; pictures of his own family hang modestly in the Morning Room.

With the damp schoolchildren sitting around him, Chris recounted these stories and pointed out the portraits of the protagonists. He had his listeners guessing about the identity and purpose of a polished tea-poy standing elegant on its single leg, and showed them the secrets of the Queen Anne bureau-bookcase; made of exquisite burr yew, the bureau is a marvel of ingenious craftsmanship, hiding a Chinese puzzle's worth of secret drawers and private compartments. The children were fascinated and fell to discussing what secrets might have been hidden in the deepest recesses of the bureau.

When even these wonders ran out, Chris resorted to quizzing the children to see how much they had remembered from their guided tour that morning; the amount of information they had retained astonished him. The time flew by, their coach returned and they departed, leaving us with the pleasing feeling that they had really gained something from their visit.

## Fishing at Felbrigg Lake

The middle of June sees the beginning of the fishing season. We allow twelve rods a day on our lake, from dawn to dusk, and naturally the first day is much sought-after by enthusiasts. Usually, to be fair to all, names are drawn out of a hat for this particular day. However, the lake is popular all through the season and for weeks beforehand the phone is busy with calls to book spaces. Tickets, which should be obtained before starting to fish, are available at the front desk during open hours.

Newcomers buying fishing tickets often return after some while to enquire with perplexity as to the exact whereabouts of the lake. They have searched everywhere and can't even *see* any water. Actually the lake is only a few hundred yards away in front of the Hall, across a field full of cows, but it's hidden in a hollow. All you can see from the Hall are the trees on its far bank—except from the vantage point of the roof, from where part of the water's surface is visible. The lake is reached via a beautiful, if in places marshy, lakeside walk among trees and across fields, though there is closer access for fishermen, once they know where to find it.

Naturally, as with most things, the fishing season brought its own complications, at all hours. One man wanted to call for his tickets at 4 a.m., just before he went to the lake to start fishing with the dawn. Others would phone, or turn up in person and ring the doorbell late in the evening prior to fishing the next day.

On the first day of that year's fishing season, neighbouring farmers complained of overnight campers in the woods by the lake, and slamming car doors which kept them from sleep. As fishing continued these complaints intensified and eventually Chris typed out a notice which he stapled to all the tickets, reminding fishermen of the 'no night fishing, no camping' rules. By law, anyway, no one should be on the estate between dusk and dawn except residents. Eventually the message got through and complaints from our neighbours lessened, though our volunteer bailiffs often reported people fishing without tickets, and litter left near the lake, not to mention potentially dangerous hooks and lengths of line carelessly discarded by the unthinking few.

## The 'Living History' Project

While routine work and small incidents continued, the main event of an early summer which was proving damp and grey for the most part, was the 'Living History' project for schools. Run by a company of local actors, this project was intended to give children a flavour of what it was like to live in the eighteenth century, by having them act out scenes and join in relevant activities. There had, of course, been letters exchanged and various meetings held over the past months in connection with the project. Now came the culmination of a year's planning.

The actors would be with us for three weeks in June, using the first week for rehearsals, perfecting their costumes and finding their way about. During the remaining two weeks, groups of children and teachers from various schools had booked places on the project—about a hundred and twenty were expected each weekday. The actors had to liaise closely with house staff to ensure that they did not interfere with the everyday running of the Hall and the pleasure of our other visitors.

The plan was for them to use certain rooms of the Hall in the mornings, before we opened, then to be out of doors from lunchtime on, rehearsing a masque whose performance would mark the end of their day. In case of rain, a marquee had been erected not far from the Hall.

The actors would lead the activities, playing fictional eighteenth-century characters—the lord and his steward would be in the Library; the lady and her maid in one of the bedrooms; the priest and his school in the Morning Room; the cook in a 'kitchen' improvised in the cellars; the gamekeeper about the estate. . . . Groups of children and teachers, dressed in suitable costume, would attend each of these principles, and minor dramas were planned to add to the excitement every day—an irate "tenant" would come to the Hall demanding to see the lord, protesting about enclosures of common land; a poacher would be caught stealing game; and an old gipsy woman was to be dragged in front of the lord and put in the stocks for begging.

During the first 'rehearsal' week, the actors were in the Hall every morning, finding their way about and learning what was feasible and what was not allowed. They decked the cellar out as a kitchen, with straw on the floor, a big table, baskets of logs, bunches of herbs. Down there, the cook's group would prepare a snack lunch for the whole gathering—simple things like bread rolls, carrots, and apples.

With so many children expected to be moving in groups from area to area of Hall and grounds as their own part of the action proceeded, we needed help directing traffic. Two of our room guides, a husband and wife, kindly volunteered for this duty and turned up suitably clad, the wife in apron and mob cap, the husband in breeches and cravat. Another lady was manning the front desk, since the door had to be open for the actors' convenience but other visitors were not allowed into the house during the morning. She too appeared in long skirts and mob cap. The staff were supposed to blend in with the eighteenth-century atmosphere which the actors were trying to create.

Trying to help, Chris offered to don a sheet and do a 'ghost' appearance to add an extra dimension for the children. The offer was not taken up.

The project did, however, provide one or two moments of hilarity, especially on the first day when the actor playing the irate tenant came storming up to the courtyard demanding to see 'Mr Windham'. His costume could have passed for modern casual dress, so the lady on the front desk mistook him for a

A case of mistaken identity at the front door

genuine complainant and started trying to mollify him. He, in turn, took her for one of his acting team, and stayed in character to continue his harangue. Since the action was, anyway, largely extemporised, a crazy cross-purposes conversation ensued. Witnesses, including the 'lord' and his 'steward' watching from the Library above, were much too busy laughing to interfere.

The children, when they arrived, were charmingly decked out in a varying semblance of costume, anything their ingenious parents could devise—the girls in long skirts and aprons, some with caps, the boys in open-necked shirts with scarves knotted about their throats and socks pulled up over trousers—and with their feet in the inevitable trainers. They flitted about the house, trailing behind costumed actors who were all deeply into character. Some of the children took it very seriously, too, their faces intent; others couldn't resist a few giggles.

Every day brought a fresh batch of children, from schools all across the region. The vast majority were well-behaved and caused us no trouble at all. Sad to say, it was a few of the teachers who let them down. They grew bored and took to exploring, opening cupboards, drawers and doors marked Private, riffling through books and handling delicate porcelain and glassware, ignoring frequent notices which implored 'Please do not touch'.

The actors themselves were not immune from this syndrome. Though asked not to touch things other than those which had been specifically designated for their use, they seemed to forget that they were in a privileged position. One of them filled a scent bottle with perfume, ignoring the possible corrosive effect on the silver top and the fact that it was very old and delicate; another kept sneaking off to the toilet to have a cigarette—the smell of smoke betrayed him, drifting along adjacent corridors; others dropped food in the corridors and trampled it about; and every day there was straw littered about near the door from the cellars.

Some of these problems were to be expected, but they did create more work for our staff, whose job it was to present the house in the best possible way. Chris and his helpers tried to keep an eye on everyone during the mornings' acting sessions, and at lunchtimes when actors and children moved outside he had to scurry about tidying up before afternoon visitors arrived.

Just before noon—if all went to plan—the children, actors and teachers issued forth from the Hall and made for the marquee to have their picnic lunch. The cooks and their little côterie of kitchen maids and scullions carried baskets full of bread, fruit, carrots and whatever other snacks they had prepared that day. Weather permitting, they spent the afternoon on the lawns in the walled garden, playing old-fashioned games and rehearsing their 'masque' for performance at the end of the day. Their activities provided an extra diversion for our afternoon visitors.

Another aspect of this 'Living History' project was the farm animals, borrowed by the acting team from various friends and imported to paddocks and pasture behind the Hall. The actor designated "farmer" was staying in a caravan parked on the car park, in order to look after his livestock. In one enclosure two ponies grazed; in another mooched a cow and her calf; a pen confined a sheep and two lambs, with goats for neighbours, and a wire run held chickens. When we went for our evening stroll, we visited the animals and took pleasure in their company, which rather upset our own resident donkeys, who seemed to think that tid-bits and strokes were their sole prerogative.

The 'Living History' events took place only on weekdays, so at the weekend there were no schoolchildren, or actors, about, though the Hall was open as usual. On a Saturday evening Chris and I took a walk in the gardens to say hello to the livestock, only to discover that the ponies were out of their paddock; someone had left the gate unfastened. We rounded up the animals and shut them in.

The cow, in her enclosure with her calf tethered to a tree, was very friendly and came to be petted. She nuzzled Chris's chest, licking persistently at his sweater, which made him wonder if she might be thirsty since her water container was dry.

Going to the stand-pipe in the stable yard, he brought back a full bucket, the sight of which agitated the cow; she couldn't wait to get her head in the bucket, so much so that Chris had a struggle to fill the old tin bath from which she was meant to drink. She was incredibly thirsty. Her calf, too, was beginning to cry and strain at its tether. We poured some more water for it and the pair drank greedily, only beginning to slow down four buckets later. How long was it since they had been watered?

The actor supposedly looking after the livestock was not in his caravan, nor did he appear all evening. In his absence, Chris kept an eye on the animals and reported the incident to the leader of the project when he returned. There was nothing else he could do since neither actors nor animals were, officially, his responsibility.

Unofficially, *everything* that happens in the Hall and its environs may become the responsibility of house staff. We never know what will happen next.


One grey and rainy morning, when actors and children were well into their sessions, the fire alarm sounded. Instantly, everything stopped.

Actors and staff followed their instructions for such emergencies and cleared the house. Swiftly, quietly, without any fuss at all, the entire company of children, teachers, actors, and National Trust staff assembled in the grass courtyard in the rain; though some had come from distant areas such as bedrooms and cellars, the house was completely cleared in less than two minutes—a pleasing result for all concerned.

Meanwhile, Chris and Robert were checking the source of the alarm—it proved to be the Morning Room, where the 'school' was being held. There was no fire and when the alarms were checked they reset without trouble. We concluded that the schoolmaster had been a little too vigorous in rubbing his blackboard clean of chalk; the sudden flurry of chalk-dust in the air had set off the smoke detectors.

When the 'Living History' project finally ended, the Morning Room was covered in a film of white dust, the removal of which kept Chris busy in spare moments for several days (and the residue of which is still apparent four years later in a fine film that collects on the concert chairs and has to be dusted off every time they are to be used). We also found some minor damages to the fabric and contents of the house. Was it all worth it? Fortunately, that was for others to decide.

At the end of the month, we snatched a few days' much-needed break before the deadline which forbids house staff to take holidays during July and August, the busiest months. At other times when the house is open we may take a few days together if work permits, but longer breaks are possible only in the 'closed' season, which in practice means January and February; in March there is usually too much to be done preparing for opening.

However, a short break before we plunged into the really busy weeks was welcome. It refreshed us ready for the onslaught of the main tourist season which lay ahead.

## Another Opening, Another Show

On two consecutive high-summer Fridays, performances of a special costumed extravaganza were to take place, in the form of a musical play set in a Victorian drawing room, where hosts and guests would allow themselves to be persuaded to perform their party pieces. The concert was being organised by a group of talented local amateurs.

Because of restricted space in the Morning Room—the usual concert room—both performances were to be held in the Dining Room. This, of course, meant that the Dining Room's furniture had to be moved out yet again, to create space for seventy concert chairs which were to be transported from the Morning Room.

Chris completed his preparatory work on Friday morning, arranging the chairs in rows, and after lunch the concert artistes and their helpers arrived to set up their own props. These included spotlights, a clavichord, string instruments, music stands and other set-dressing paraphernalia. Even in the Dining Room there was not really enough space for the performers to spread out as they might have liked, so compromises had to be made.

Some of the artistes were not happy at having to amend their plans and there were a few disagreements, especially over the placing of the spotlights. In a position which would suit the artistes, the lights, which would get hot during the performance, were much too near our precious paintings. Chris made sure they were placed where they could cause no damage, but every time he left the room the lights were moved back, apparently because the scene setters thought he was being unnecessarily fussy. Every time he returned, he was forced to re-argue the point. Artistic preferences conflicted with his duty to protect the house, but minor arguments were probably inevitable with so many people to please and such varying concerns to be accommodated. Eventually all was ready and final rehearsals began.

Apart from the change of venue, the concert routine followed as usual. With the help of a volunteer or two from our pool of

The battle of the spotlight

room wardens, Chris and I welcomed the audience in, taking tickets, directing people to order interval drinks, generally doing 'front of house' duty until everyone was settled and Robert could make his usual introductory speech. The artistes appeared in their costumes, adrenalin running high, and to anticipatory applause the concert began. We slipped away to eat.

During the interval, Chris noticed that one of the spotlights was still too close to a painting—it must have been moved just before the concert began, when he was too busy to notice. The light was off when he did see it, but it had been blazing away for an hour, inches from an irreplaceable Windham portrait which still felt warm to the touch. Naturally he returned the light to a safer place; it might mean that someone hadn't got his full share of limelight, but that had to be weighed against causing irreparable damage. In this instance, the safety of the painting was paramount.

At the end of the evening, the slight contention forgotten, most of the crew pitched in and helped to carry the concert chairs back to the Morning Room, for which Chris and I were grateful. We spent the rest of a very long evening—ending near midnight —reinstating the Dining Room furniture. We might have left it until the morning, but come the morning Chris had plenty to do cleaning lavatories and restaurant/kitchen floors in the wake of the concert-goers, besides performing all his usual duties in preparation for another 'Open to the public' afternoon.

A week later, the same pattern repeated for the second performance of the show, but this time the artistes seemed to appreciate that we did understand and sympathise with their requirements even though our over-riding concern had to be with the welfare of the house.

The special concerts were a great success. Both audiences seemed thoroughly to enjoy their evening.

Routine work carried on as usual, the mornings busy with the cleaners at their work requiring supervision and occasional help with heavy jobs; deliveries, workmen in, visits from architects, surveyors, builders' reps, not to mention personnel from regional office calling on their various concerns.

A new variation was the arrival of several sets of contractors coming to see the roof, which was in urgent need of re-leading. They all had to be escorted up through the attics and shown the relevant areas; later they would tender their contracts for the work—a project for the coming winter.

Small emergencies continued to occur nearly every day: pipes got blocked, taps leaked and cisterns overflowed; faults occurred in the electricity supply, or the alarms; gadgets and machinery failed in various ways; drawers stuck, pieces of plasterwork came off, hinges broke. . . . Scarcely a day went by without raising some extra job to be done, and on five afternoons a week the Hall was open, with consequent duties and problems flowing one into the other.

## Callers

In order to save two people running to answer the same phone or doorbell, these jobs were divided: as a rule, Robert answered phones and Chris answered doors. Of course, when either was away the other had to do both, if humanly possible—or a wife might come in handy as a temporary telephonist.

Some days the phone brought interminable enquiries about fishing tickets, booked lunches, coach parties and the inevitable —"Can you tell me what times you are open, please?"

People call at the strangest hours, whenever it happens to suit them, from 7.30 in the morning to late at night; if we ask them to call back during normal office hours, because officially the Hall is closed after 6 at night, we often hear a surprised, "But your number's here in the book!"


Closed days, which for us are the equivalent of other people's weekends, are sometimes particularly busy. During that first summer there were the two musical evenings, both on Fridays, and on another Friday we had a special opening to accommodate a visit from staff of another property where Robert was previously based. They lingered until nearly 7 o'clock.

On a Monday, we helped Joan and her staff to deck the restaurant out as if for Christmas, complete with tree, trimmings, and a festive table laid with crackers. Everyone available was called in to act as a party-goer while a photographer shot several rolls of film. He was preparing a promotional feature for use nearer Christmastime, to advertise the Christmas lunches we were planning to offer for the first time that year. It was great fun to be involved all together in this sociable way, despite the work involved in setting it all up and later taking it all down. Still, it was in a good cause.

Or was it? Four years on, we're still wondering whatever became of those photographs. We never did see a sign of them!

## The Gardens

On yet another Friday we had one of our biannual special garden openings which are part of the National Gardens' Scheme. Proceeds from these days go to a nursing charity. One of our regular ticket-sellers was positioned in a wooden hut near the garden entrance; she charged an entry fee of fifty pence, even to members of the National Trust since this is a 'special opening' for another charity. The gardens were at their best now, ablaze with summer colour, especially the many varieties of roses. And, for the convenience of visitors to the gardens, we also opened the shop and the restaurant.

Chris kept an eye on all areas during the afternoon, frequently walking across the pasture to visit the ticket-seller and lend moral support. The weather was disappointing, damp and dull, with not very many people about; but the ticket-seller is a cheerful, obliging lady; she refused to get down-hearted.

The gardens around the Hall are rich with blossoming shrubs and trees, gravelled walks and wide areas of lawn kept smooth by our head gardener, Ted, and his assistant Mark, with the help of a young apprentice: three of them—one wonders how many gardeners the same area employed in its hey-day. Our own three garden staff work long hard hours all round the year; their efforts produce magnificent results.

Behind the Orangery lie shaded walks where rhododendrons of every hue from creamy white to deepest purple, through lilac, magenta and lush pinks grow alongside the vivid sunset glow of azaleas. Passing along, you reach the cool dark aisle of the American Garden with its tall pines growing in strange twisted shapes; where their branches touch the ground, they have rooted and their inverted arches form natural seats in a green glade. From there, follow the path across a stretch of pasture, where children love to stop and feed sugar to the donkeys in their paddock. Past a wondrous twisted, ancient sweet chestnut you reach the gate of the Walled Garden, arched over by the branches of an old walnut tree.

Beyond the gate, the scents of the Walled Garden will greet you—sharp tang of box hedges, sweetness of lilies and roses, the many fragrances of the herb garden. Clematis and figs grow against the walls, alongside pears and cherries. Bees drone from their hives in long wildflower-tangled grass where frogs hide beneath apple trees. In soft-fruit cages raspberries and goose-berries hang thickly in season, and with them currants both black and red. An armless merman presides over a pool where water-lilies spread vast cups of cream, yellow and crimson-streaked pink; there are greenhouses where mimosa grows, and hot-house flowers, and vines, and citrus fruits. And over it all lifts the dove-house, where white doves still breed. Disturbed, they lift with a clatter of wings from the wooden tiles of the dove-house roof to swirl in dazzling arcs against a blue sky and float down to strut on the lawns.

When the National Trust took over the care of the estate, the walled garden was in a neglected condition. Now, it is a verdant bower set amid acres of parkland, where each season brings fresh beauty.

With the holiday season in full swing, some of our room guides were going away too, leaving gaps in the daily schedules. Others of our volunteers very kindly filled in where they could, and of course I was always nearby when help was needed, either for a full afternoon's duty or to act as tea relief—or to fill any other gap that might arise.

Our younger son, Kevin, living nearby in Norwich, was a frequent visitor, often bringing with him a gaggle of his nursing friends. He too would stand in as a room guide if needed. And if nothing else could be found to occupy him and his friends they could always help Robert by taking energetic bull-terrier Sam for one of his twice-daily walks. With Felbrigg's vast park and woodlands just beyond the door, that was no hardship for the youngsters.

Kevin had taken a great fancy to the country life. He is also a keen fisherman and couldn't wait to sink a hook into Felbrigg lake. One weekend, having booked tickets for fishing, he and a friend arrived late at night. They intended to be up early, to tramp across the fields to the lake as dawn broke.

"You must be mad," said Chris. "Just be sure to bring us a few fish for supper. What—you throw them back into the water? Then what's the point of going?" He was teasing, of course. Kevin refused to rise to the bait; we hoped the fish would be more obliging.

The young men left at 4 in the morning, unheard by either of us.

And a few hours later the party of teenagers from Germany arrived to stay in the base camp over the stable block for three weeks.

## The Germans

'The Germans', as they were collectively called by everyone at the Hall, were a party of young people who had come to enjoy a holiday in Norfolk. Their leader had brought a group to Felbrigg in previous years and the tenants told colourful tales of sins committed and friendships made on earlier occasions. We were reserving judgement: let us wait and see what happened *this* year.

They seemed a pleasant bunch of teenagers, mixed boys and girls, about ten of each, with their leader, Ralf, and a couple of other slightly older supervisors. They had travelled by road and North Sea ferry, in a minibus which soon acquired the title 'The Panzerwagen'. It was crammed with their belongings, including what seemed like tons of food to keep them going during their three-week stay.

When they arrived, Chris went to show them their quarters and go through the usual base-camp routine, getting them settled in with instructions about the fire escapes, parking, milk deliveries, and anything else that would help them be comfortable and fit in with everyone at the Hall. He spoke enough German to hold a conversation and even make a few jokes, thus establishing a rapport and helping to make the newcomers feel more at home.

Having been to Felbrigg before, Ralf knew his way about and had made plans to amuse his companions with outings and activities. Most of the time we expected them to be self-sufficient, though naturally we should bump into them in the stable yard for a chat now and then, and in a real emergency they were welcome to come and ring the bell of the Green Door.

That very first night, at about 10 o'clock, a few of them came trooping across the courtyard below our flat. When they rang the bell, Chris leaned from a window to see what had brought them.

"Ve haf an emergency!" one of them declared.

"What's wrong?" Chris asked in concern.

"Ve haf no salt!"

They were supplied with salt, and a little pep talk on the nature of emergencies.

Though the base campers were generally well-behaved and courteous they were also young and exuberant, away from parental authority. After a few days, stories began to filter through to us—via tenants who lived adjacent to the base camp —of noisy goings-on late at night, lasting until as late as 4 in the morning, lights off and on at all hours, and spitting contests taking place from the parapet; the fact that one of the tenants happened to be walking below at the time was, we trust, coincidental. He had made no official complaint, but the incident obviously upset him and Chris asked Ralf to control his charges a little better. After that, things quietened down for a while.

One of the boys of the group was seen hobbling about with his foot wrapped up. It appeared he had one night decided it might be fun to jump from the parapet—a good fifteen feet high —into the gravelled stable yard. Whether he had been drinking at the time remained a moot point, but whatever the cause of this crazy feat it resulted in a damaged ankle. Had he seen a doctor? No, Ralf didn't think that was necessary. No amount of persuasion could change his mind, but the young man hobbled for the rest of his holiday. We could only hope he hadn't broken a bone and done permanent damage.

Next the 'Panzerwagen' developed trouble with its battery and we heard they were having problems starting it up. One day Ralf had the vehicle in the stable yard, its bonnet up and his head inside. He told Chris, who happened to be passing, that the battery was not charging properly, but he declined an offer to charge it up since part of his group needed the vehicle straight away for a planned outing. Whatever he was doing under the bonnet evidently worked—the minibus was seen driving away.

Later that same day, Tom, our head woodsman, informed Chris that the electric fence around the cattle field had been vandalised—its battery was missing. It didn't take a genius to work out where the battery might have gone. Chris was very annoyed and went to find Ralf who, with a few of his people, had remained behind while the rest went out for the day.

"How did you get the van going?" Chris asked. "You didn't steal the battery from the fence, did you?"

Ralf looked horrified. "Steal? No, no—we only borrowed it!"

"You took it without permission. That's stealing."

The word filled Ralf with guilt. He protested that they meant no harm: they were in a hurry; they meant only to *borrow* the battery.

"That's not the point," said Chris. "Not only did you take the battery but now the electric fence isn't working and the cattle can get out. They'll cause havoc if they stray on to the road. I'm afraid you're all going to have to stand along the fence and shoo the cows away if they come too close. We can't have them getting out of the field. They're valuable cattle.''

Contrite and consternated, Ralf gathered his remaining forces and posted them at intervals along the currentless fence. Every time a cow so much as looked at them, they waved their arms and cried, "Shoo! Shoo!" or the German equivalent.

The Germans, atoning for transgressions

Now, cows are inquisitive creatures. The herd, which had been scattered widely across the field, mostly on the far side well away from the fence, began to move across to see what all the fuss and noise was about. The nearer they came, the more frantic grew the shooing, only increasing the cows' interest. They wouldn't come too near, of course—cows are nervous as well as curious—but they approached, *en masse*, near enough to have the base campers dashing about in desperate efforts to make them go away.

The teenagers were all mightily relieved when their friends, and the van, returned and the fence battery could be refixed. The fence being 'live' again, the cow-wards relaxed, having atoned for their transgressions by providing a little amusement for the rest of us.

The Norfolk Broads, some twenty miles distant, offered an interesting venue for the base campers to enjoy themselves. Ralf had apparently hired a boat, or so we were informed by the tenants who lived off the stable yard and therefore saw most of the youngsters. We also heard that our visitors had been in trouble because of illegal mooring, but fortunately that was not our concern; it was probably a misunderstanding, anyway.

It was not really our concern, either, when a phone call from one of the group informed us that their vehicle had broken down yet again. Ralf had managed to get it to a garage, but it would be out of commission for a while and meanwhile the fifteen or so teenagers who had gone on the Broads that day were stranded at Wroxham. No, it was not our concern, strictly speaking, but we could hardly leave them to walk twenty miles on their own. Chris told them to stay where they were and he would come. Although he was in the middle of his evening meal when the call came through, he set out at once to rescue the unfortunates. The mission took all evening—three trips, a drive of over a hundred miles in all.

The grateful Ralf wanted to pay for the petrol used, but we knew the group was short of funds so Chris told him not to worry, we were glad to help. However, the Germans didn't leave it at that; a day or two later they rang our private bell and presented Chris with a beautiful illustrated book on country houses, and a box of chocolates for me.

Another hare was started when Robert spotted a 'tent' in the woods, and asked Chris to investigate. Camping on Felbrigg estate is not allowed. However, the tent in the woods was not for camping: it was a mock-up, part of the 'set' for a video film which our young visitors had been making—the story of Robin Hood and his Merry Men, apparently. Now that their vehicle was in for repair they were less mobile, so the video became their main activity, providing hours of entertainment for us, too, as we watched them stage various scenes. Their 'costumes' were basic: Robin Hood had a green cap with a jaunty feather, but the tunics of his merry men were blue plastic dustbin liner bags with head- and arm-holes cut in them. Beneath these, pale young legs dangled, ending incongruously in dark socks and trainers. Led by Robin, this motley band of outlaws was filmed marching up and down in front of the Hall one evening, singing a stirring song—in German, of course.

On another day, my sister who was staying with us and sharing the fun spied one of the German boys near the church, wearing a sack stuffed with a cushion.

"Ah—Friar Tuck, yes?"

A wide grin. "*Ja! Ja!*" He didn't speak much English but he was delighted to be identified in his role.

Really they were an engaging crowd and we grew very fond of them as the three weeks progressed. Sadly, their 'Panzer-wagen' was declared beyond repair and they had to abandon it.

On their last evening they appeared again at our door, laden with all kinds of foodstuffs which they couldn't take back with them now that they had no vehicle. They wanted us to have it, but, no, they wouldn't take any payment for it, it was useless to them now and if we couldn't use it they would throw it away. Bags of flour, huge blocks of cheese, enormous tubs of margarine . . . we wondered if they had been expecting a siege. Judging from the German-style packaging, they must have brought most of the stuff with them. Perhaps they didn't trust British food. Since there was far too much for us to use ourselves, we donated much of it for the use of the restaurant, though we did keep some. A drum of drinking chocolate lasted us for months, and a giant pot of paprika still resides in our cupboard, hardly touched and years past its 'use before' date.

On inspecting the base camp with Ralf just before the visitors finally left, Chris found it spotless. The youngsters had worked very hard to clean every corner and had even mended a couple of broken chairs for us.

For many reasons, we shall never forget our friends the Germans.

## All on a Summer's Day

It was high summer, but torrential rains poured down for several days. Water seeped through various places in the roof, fully demonstrating its need for urgent repair, and drove past the Jacobean leads of the windows in some of the state rooms. Cloths were laid to mop up the excess. As for the roof, plans for its renovation were underway but couldn't be carried out for months yet. Temporary measures had to be employed. When the weather was bad, it was necessary for Chris to make frequent forays on to the roof to make sure the gullies remained open, and when the leaks became an urgent problem he spent one morning of deluge getting drenched out there with builders who hoped to supply a temporary answer.

Meanwhile, the Hall was at its busiest. In the tourist area around us camping and caravan sites, boarding houses and hotels were full. All of these visitors were looking for things to do, especially when bad weather barred them from the beaches. Consequently, some days in the height of the season were hectic.

Take one particular August Wednesday. . . .

While finishing an early breakfast, we heard an alarm klaxon which sent Chris rushing all the way from our flat, through the restaurant and corridors, to the fire panel, only to realise as his head cleared that the 'fire alarm' was no longer sounding. Robert hadn't appeared, either, as he always did every time an alarm sounded. The panel was quiescent, all lights at green. Come to think of it, the sound hadn't come from the roof where the siren was situated—it seemed to have come from the grass courtyard outside our flat. What was going on?

Investigating, Chris encountered Ted, the head gardener, who confessed to being responsible for the noise. He had borrowed a motor horn, in order to play a wake-up trick on his assistant, who lives in one of the apartments off the courtyard. It wasn't until he had sounded the horn that he realised just how loud it would be. We all laughed about it, of course, but Ted was most apologetic and later brought a gift of delicious plums from trees in the Walled Garden.

His joke had, anyway, got Chris moving with time to enjoy a most beautiful morning, a change after days of downpour. As he opened up the Hall, he paused for a while in the Rose Garden to look at the view. Across the pasture as the sun climbed, a mist was lifting from the lake, drifting into a blue sky trimmed with wisps of cloud. A flight of geese took off, honking, heading for feeding grounds on the salt marshes along the coast. A newborn calf was struggling to its feet, watched by its anxious mother, while the rest of the herd were scattered, browsing contentedly. As Chris breathed in the freshness of the air a pair of Egyptian geese swooped in to land on the pasture, their broad, dark-tipped wings brilliant white in the early sunlight.

Another movement drew his attention to where, appearing from nowhere, a honey buzzard flew to perch on the iron fence surrounding the front courtyard. Chris had seen the bird before, but had never been privileged with such a close view, and this time the female had her chick with her, almost grown. She flew down to where a puddle lay in the gravel courtyard, a legacy of recent rains. Apparently she was demonstrating the art of bathing, hoping that her offspring would take the hint, but though she repeated the process several times, flying to the fence and down again to splash more water over her feathers, the chick remained unimpressed. After a while, the pair flew away and only then did an entranced Chris move to continue opening shutters and unlocking doors, readying the Hall for another day.

Soon the world came crowding in to dispel the idyll. At 8.30 the cleaners were at the back door, immediately starting on their regular routine of dusting furniture, vacuum-cleaning druggets and cleaning lavatories. Chris stayed near the door; he was expecting Peter, the shop manager, to arrive ready to handle one of the regular deliveries for the shop from the National Trust central depot at Melksham—a delivery which was scheduled for 8.30. Peter arrived on time. The delivery did not.

While waiting, ready to unlock the Green Door when necessary, Chris took the chance to hammer some tacks into the carpet on the office stairs, which are steep and narrow enough without

118

the added hazard of loose carpeting. Peter found things to do in the shop.

Before Chris had finished fixing the carpet, one of the cleaners came with news that the big 'wet and dry' vacuum cleaner had packed up—oh, and incidentally the wash basins in the gents' cloakroom were blocked.

This problem took priority; it had to be dealt with before the restaurant and cloakrooms opened at noon, though it meant that Chris would have to be in part of the house where he couldn't easily hear the doorbell. If the delivery from Melksham arrived now the driver would have to wait—he was already nearly half an hour late and the business of the Hall couldn't mark time until he came.

Having tried to unblock the washbasins manually, Chris went to a distant store room and found some caustic soda, but as he was making for the gents' again he heard the doorbell and detoured to answer it. No, it was not the expected delivery, it was two workmen arriving unannounced to replace the flooring in the base camp. They had to be taken across to the stable block and shown where they needed to be. While they made a start on their work, Chris returned to the gents' with the caustic soda. With a good deal of poking and prodding, eventually the blockage moved and the water drained freely again.

By this time Peter had left; he had other business to attend to before he opened the shop at 12, so if the Melksham lorry came in his absence it would be up to Chris to see the delivery safely into the store rooms.

His next immediate task was to phone the vacuum cleaner firm and ask for someone to come and take a look at the machine; it was a useful tool whose absence would be missed, so it had to be back in service as soon as possible.

While he was on the phone, the doorbell rang again, and again, persistently and impatiently. He rushed down the narrow office stairs, nearly breaking his neck when his shoe caught in the fraying carpet, and discovered a woman outside, elegantly garbed in linen suit and spiky heels. She had, she informed him, brought a delivery for the shop, though she had left the boxes in her car in the stable yard.

"If you bring them in, I'll show you where they go," Chris offered, thinking that while he was waiting he could finish tacking the stair carpet, before someone—himself, probably—had an accident.

But the woman regarded him as if he had turned blue. "You don't expect *me* to carry them, do you? There are three boxes!"

"You could make three trips," he suggested. "Or you can borrow a sack barrow, if you like."

"Look, *I'm* certainly not carting them all the way across here!" she responded. "If you want them, you'll have to come and get them. Otherwise I shall just leave them in the stable yard. You can't expect *me* to carry three heavy boxes all the way across here."

So much for women's lib.

It was now 10.30. As Chris stowed the boxes away, having fetched them on the light sack barrow, he decided it was time for a break; but before he could make for the stairs to our flat Robert emerged from the office with a letter he had just received —a letter concerning the portable case of books which is displayed on one of the tables in the Library.

This small, glass-fronted case, containing two shelves full of slim leather-bound volumes, had for some time been confidently referred to as a 'carriage library'; such artifacts were designed, so we were assured by the room wardens (though where this information originated was not quite clear), to be taken on journeys by gentlemen who might fancy having something to read while travelling in their conveyance. It didn't sound entirely plausible that a glass-fronted case, easily broken if it were dropped, would be designed for use in a carriage, but that seemed to be the accepted explanation.

Now, a lady had written with further information: on a recent visit to the Hall she had been delighted to see that we had a 'Servants' Library'. She had spoken to Chris about it and promised that she would send further details. Her letter informed us that such libraries are well documented and were usually stocked with copies of twenty-five particular books, of which she enclosed a list of titles—titles such as *Pilgrim's Progress*, *Call to the Unconverted*, *The Faithful Servant*, *Waste Not*, *Want Not*—*Sarah and her Mistress*, *The Careful Nursemaid*, *The Parables Explained* and so on—all moral and uplifting tracts just perfect for the edification of one's servants.

Asked to check this information, Chris discovered that the correspondent was perfectly right about the titles of the books. The previous thinking on the 'carriage library' was obviously incorrect. Later, when time allowed, he wrote an explanatory note on the subject, putting a copy in the room folder as an *aide-mémoire* for whichever warden might be in the Library when someone asked about the case of books.

Old habits persisted, however. We later heard one of the room wardens telling visitors that the little case of books was, "a 'servants' library'—designed to be taken in carriages".

The August day wore on. Tempting aromas floated from the restaurant, where Joan and her staff were preparing lunches. His appetite stirred, Chris was coming up to the flat for his belated coffee break—the route lies through the restaurant—when one of the waitresses stopped him for a chat and before he could get away the doorbell rang yet again. This time it was a salesman hoping to persuade our shop to buy his wares; no, he hadn't made an appointment, he had just thought he would call in while passing. If the shop manager wasn't available, perhaps Chris would like to . . .

Chris wouldn't—the merchandise in the shop is one thing that is *not* in the province of house staff.

At 11.20, he finally made it to the flat, where I was busy on my latest epic; he offered to make me a coffee, too, while he was about it, but before the kettle could boil the doorbell rang again —it was firmly connected with our flat, among other places. The Melksham delivery had arrived, nearly three hours late.

By the time Chris had seen the numerous boxes safely into the store room it was hardly worth his trying for a coffee break since lunchtime loomed. He spent the intervening minutes straightening piles of leaflets and checking notice boards, exchanging pleasantries with the restaurant staff as they came to and from their store.

Just before noon he secured the house, leaving access only to restaurant, shop and cloakrooms, then as the courtyard clock struck the hour he unlocked the Rose Garden door and walked to the front courtyard to open the gates for lunchers who had already formed a small queue. Only then did he realise that the glorious morning had clouded over. The sky looked threatening.

Sure enough, as we ate lunch the deluge started and by the time Chris was changing into his more formal afternoon clothes we heard a mutter of thunder.

1.15 p.m.: Chris began his afternoon routine of opening blinds and preparing the rooms for our volunteers and visitors. Shortly after 1.30 he joined Robert in the Morning Room where the room wardens for the day were gathering, chattering noisily, sharing witticisms and remarks about the awful weather—in August, too. Typical British summer!

"Couldn't you have organised it better than this, Chris?" someone joked. "I nearly got washed away coming down the path."

One by one they were checked off on Robert's list and informed of the expected parties—three separate coachloads had booked for different times that day.

It turned out to be a chaotic afternoon. The bad weather brought people in droves, seeking shelter. Soon after opening, the ticket-seller's desk and the inner lobby became the repository for a dozen wet umbrellas.

Taking a break from my word-processor—an excuse for me to see what was happening and have a chat—I was in time to see a couple come in soaking wet to collect their umbrellas. The exit door is some distance from the front door and, with rain streaming down, the walk between meant that everyone leaving a brolly at the desk got soaked coming to retrieve it. I offered to transfer umbrellas, via a private passageway, to the recruiter's desk near the exit. The recruiter promised to keep an eye on them until their owners collected them—*before* venturing out into the downpour.

At the time, I must confess, I hadn't anticipated just how many visitors would take advantage of this kind offer, so that soon I was running a shuttle service for umbrellas, wet macs, anoraks, even a couple of pushchairs. Sometimes I'm a fool to myself. Still, it was worth it for the grateful words and smiles of our

The shuttle service

visitors. They were able to set off on their tour of the house unencumbered and happy, forgetting about the weather. Happily, the articles were all collected one by one as the afternoon progressed, each apparently reunited with its proper owner.

At about 2.30, a party of thirty ladies of the Women's Institute arrived. They had pre-booked, and thankfully arrived on time, so Chris was on hand to assist the ticket-seller. A few of the party were members of the Trust and, assuming they had their cards with them, could enter for free; the rest needed tickets, for which their organiser had brought a cheque; then the tickets had to be distributed, and guide books or leaflets sold. With thirty ladies all trying to cram into the lobby out of the rain, crowding round the desk, asking questions, holding out money for books, leaving umbrellas . . . for a few minutes we were almost overwhelmed.

One of the other parties came early, the third arrived late, coinciding with an unexpected coachload of elderly people whose planned seaside outing had been ruined by the weather and so they had decided to come to us instead. Bodies crowded the lobby, which was steaming up with condensation from wet clothes and umbrellas. But somehow the ticket-seller coped and kept smiling, helping to keep our visitors' spirits up, so that most of them made a joke of the difficulties.

All afternoon, Chris was kept busy moving from point to point, solving small problems, answering visitors' queries, supplying more guide books to the desk, directing people to cloak-rooms and tea-room, preventing photographers from using cameras, providing change for the busy shop, restaurant and ticket desk, and in between whiles trying to keep an eye on the front courtyard where only disabled drivers are supposed to park, though on such a filthy day others inevitably decided to ignore the notices. Chris did what he could against near-impossible odds and I too helped wherever I saw a need.

Meanwhile in the Old Kitchen the restaurant staff were overwhelmed by work and dishes began to pile high. Joan came to find me with a plea for help, so I stopped being assistant house-man and became kitchen-maid for the afternoon. This involved stacking dirty crockery in plastic trays, and loading and unloading the dishwasher—a simple task, except that the dishwasher stood on the ground, entailing much bending and lifting. "This kitchen was obviously designed by a man who wasn't going to have to work in it," was Joan's comment. After three hours of it, I began to wonder if my aching back would ever straighten again and the rest of the staff had sore feet and frayed nerves. Still, the customers were all served, even if some of them were kept unavoidably waiting a while.

6.00 p.m.: at last the crowds had dispersed, the room wardens had gone home, and Chris could begin to lock up. I helped him, partly because I knew how tired he was and partly to help get the kinks out of my back. Soon after 6.30 we climbed to our flat, where I prepared supper. We looked forward to a quiet evening, but . . .

Late at night, our private phone rang—one of the tenants was reporting noises of shouting and revving engines, coming from somewhere in the woods behind the Hall. Chris set off to investigate, telling me to stay where I was and, at the first sign of any trouble, to phone the police. He sallied forth and was joined by the intrepid Gill, our neighbour who does the flowers; she was not going to let Chris go alone. The noises continued, as if drunken drivers were practising dirt-track racing in the woods. Then the sound of engines changed, revving up through the gears, and from a window I saw two cars shoot out of the woodland walk and along the drive, crashing over cattle grids at spring-bending speed.

We are always alert for anything strange, especially after dark. Parked cars on the estate are always investigated and their numbers noted. Occasionally Robert, when out walking Sam, discovered camper vans tucked away in the woods near the picnic area, with people preparing to stay overnight; they had to be moved on. And sometimes he disturbed a couple of lovers who evidently thought no one would be about at such a late hour.

This night-driving in the woods, however, was a mystery we never did solve. It ended a very tiring day.

However, along with the exhaustion—and the comedy—there were some romantic moments. During a summer concert, on a beautiful evening, Chris and I walked outside doing a security recce and taking a rare opportunity to enjoy our lovely surroundings in peace. Cows grazed across the pasture, a breeze stirred in the woods, birds sang; the sun was setting, geese were flying home, and strains of evocative music floated from the Morning Room. On the west lawn, against a backdrop of the stately home in which we are privileged to live, we waltzed . . .

We didn't hear the car coming along the drive fifty yards away, passing through the estate as so many do, just to view the scene. We were unaware that the driver had stopped. In fact, we didn't notice him until he was out of the car and taking pictures, probably unable to believe his eyes—people *waltzing on the lawn at the Hall!*

Such moments make up for a lot.

On one of Chris's Mondays off we were about to set off on a research trip in connection with a new historical novel I was planning. In our old life we often had time for such outings; now the opportunities are few. However, as we made for our car a large lorry backed up to the gateway of the stable yard, blocking our exit. The driver leapt down from his cab, a short, stocky man, overalls unzipped down to his navel displaying a fine set of bronzed pectorals. Either he had been abroad or he had a sun-lamp; he certainly hadn't brewed a tan like that in England, not that summer.

"Morning, squire!" he greeted Chris. "I've got a deep-freezer for delivery. Where does it want to be?"

Knowing that Robert was on duty alone, Chris was annoyed that a deep-freezer should have been sent with no warning whatsoever.

"Couldn't they have given us some notice?" he asked. "We're closed today. There's nobody about."

"That's nothing to do with me, squire. I just follow orders. So where do I take it?"

"You'll have to take it across the inner courtyard to the door in the corner," Chris replied. "Can you manage it on your own?"

"Sure, squire! No problem!"

Cheered by that assurance, we made for our car and our day out, but we had hardly gone two steps before the lorry driver said, "Where do I go to get some help?"

"You said you could manage on your own!" Chris reminded him.

"Well, so I can, but I shall need some help. Just get somebody to come and give me a hand. Who is there about?"

One couldn't argue with that sort of logic.

And, of course, from Felbrigg's massive house staff of exactly two there was only one person who could "give a hand" in this case, day off or not. Robert was near retiring age, and could hardly be expected to help haul a freezer which, when the driver unfastened the lorry, proved to be a chest-style monster complete with wooden frame. The driver had brought no means of transporting it—no wheeled trailer, no sack barrow. The Hall's own light-weight barrow would have crumpled under the weight. The only solution was human muscle power.

Somehow, the two men managed to carry the thing across the grass courtyard and down a long corridor. And I, concerned for my husband's well-being and inwardly fuming at yet another interruption to our free time, went with them to unlock doors and keep a watch on corners. I was intensely relieved when the freezer was finally deposited without someone bursting a blood vessel or having a heart attack.

## 5

# Autumn—The Mellowing Season

### *Help!—Relief Ticket-Seller Wanted*

Although most of the occasional deficiencies in our ranks had been fairly easy to fill, it became apparent that during a week in September a rather more serious hiatus would occur; both of our regular ticket-sellers would be on holiday at that time. There would be no one to man the front desk.

What we really needed, Chris mused out loud, was a relief ticket-seller capable of taking over in such emergencies—someone who was near at hand and prepared to fill in at short notice. He might train one of the room wardens, one or two of whom had shown an interest in the ticket-selling job, but it was hardly fair to do so when the need was so infrequent, and so unpredictable; between whiles the person would inevitably forget the necessary routines; no one would want a job like that. It would be so much easier all round if someone living at the Hall could do it—someone who wasn't restricted by the hours of another regular job—someone. . . .

In short, someone like his wife.

Though writing is, for me, a full-time profession (given the chance), Chris can be very persuasive. I'd have felt churlish if I had refused to take on this occasional duty, so I volunteered my services as stand-in ticket-seller, hoping the need wouldn't arise too often. I sat in at the desk on a couple of afternoons to learn the job in readiness for duty in September.

The week came and I was at the desk at least fifteen minutes before opening time, in order to check everything—cash float, house ticket numbers, fishing tickets and the various guide books, which all had to be counted and tallied with the daily records. Meanwhile the room wardens would arrive to gather in the Morning Room as usual. By now they were all old friends. "What, *you* on today?" one gentleman teased on seeing me behind the desk. "Really scraping the barrel, aren't they?" It's a lovely feeling when the house is about to come fully into gear.

The ticket-seller's task is to make visitors welcome, creating a first impression which hopefully will linger as they walk through the house. But first of course there are membership cards to check, various categories of tickets to sell, and several kinds of guide book and leaflet to offer. It must all be done with great accuracy, otherwise the records will be haywire at the end of the day.

Then there are things that the Trust requires us to watch for and prohibit for reasons of conservation or safety—pushchairs, which must be left in the lobby; stiletto or other sharp heels, and a recent addition to this list is bulky bags and back-packs, both rucksacks and those aluminium-framed seats which carry babies. We provide baby 'papoose' slings instead, if the baby is still small enough to use one in comfort.

If a wheelchair-bound visitor appeared, I generally leapt up and opened the door wider if I was free to do so, telling him or her how to find the 'escape route' that avoids the stairs. Or if a visitor seemed frail or had difficulty walking I would explain that there was a chair available in every room if a rest was needed—they had only to ask the room guide.

Fishermen also came to the desk wanting tickets for the lake. Our fishing season ends in September, when the shooting starts, so keen anglers were flocking to grab a last chance at the lake. It took a few minutes to check the diary, fill in the details, complete the fishing ticket and then probably have to explain where exactly the lake lay, and where parking was allowed.

If there was time, I might exhort visitors not to miss the walled garden: "The colchicums are wonderful this year," or tell fractious children that later they could see the donkeys. Often I was confronted with queries about the house, which I answered if I could; if not, I recommended that they ask the room wardens, most of whom were a great deal more knowledgeable than I.

Being on the desk can be hard work, especially on a busy day; it calls for a mixture of concentration, observation, diplomacy, mathematics, charm—and a good memory for facts and faces. To sustain the ticket-seller, about halfway through the afternoon, the person on 'tea relief' duty will deliver a welcome cup of tea and a couple of biscuits to the desk.

As the afternoon waned, so the flow of visitors lessened to a trickle. Only on rare occasions did anyone come in after 5.15. From 5 o'clock time started to drag and the last hour seemed longer than the preceding three put together. It's much more fun to be busy, as everyone agrees. The Great Hall guide wandered over to the door to chat with me, and the tea-relief would often join in. If anyone came we would spring back to the alert, but meantime we were idling, the Hall's energy winding down towards the end of another day.

To tell the truth, I thoroughly enjoyed being on the desk. It was a pleasure to be an official part of the team, something I still do when needed for an odd day or a few days at a time.

One extra 'front desk' duty that I learned by experience was to tally the total number of visitors who had been through the house that day. As the room wardens leave they all like to know how many we have had. They're all pleased if the number is high. If it's not, they try to guess the reasons for it—the weather, perhaps, or another attraction elsewhere. It's impossible to say why numbers fluctuate, or why it so often happens that one day the visitors all seem moody and out of sorts and the next they're as merry as pipits. Certainly the weather doesn't seem to affect that; rain or shine, either can happen. We continually remark on the unpredictability that adds interest to our day's duty.

So the room wardens departed, one by one, and as I finalised my accounts and completed the necessary paperwork I could hear Chris closing shutters. I ended my working day by helping him with his close-down, shuttering and barring the Red Corridor and the Bird Corridor as around me the shop and restaurant staff cleared up and left. Eventually Chris and I met in the front courtyard, bringing in 'This way' signs and the 'hedgehog' shoe brush before closing the garden gates and the main courtyard gates.

The autumn evenings were mellow with sunlight and we paused to drink it all in. The last cars were leaving the car park. Some of them belonged to room wardens and other staff, or Ted might drive by, heading home to his lodge for a cup of tea before starting his evening chores of, perhaps, watering, or completing the lawn-cutting; they would wave to us and we would wave back as peace returned and we had the place almost to ourselves again. House martins and swallows swooped after flies, though soon they would be gone too. A few of the trees were beginning to show yellow traces. Summer was definitely over.

## VIPs from America

A coach party of American tourists was expected, important people, including judges, lawyers and their wives. Their tour guide had requested a brief introductory talk before they went round the house, so Chris had been preparing notes and finding one or two unusual things for these special visitors to see. When their coach arrived, he invited them into the Morning Room where he gave them a brief grounding on the house and its history.

Since they were all people connected with the law, he had thought they might be interested to see a set of old court books he had found in the back of a cupboard. The books are relevant to a village which is described on the covers as 'Owby cum Thyrne'—some masters of the Felbrigg estates were, we discovered, also Lords of the Manor of Owby. The books start out in Latin, mostly illegible except to a Latin scholar, but they gradually turn to English in which one can pick out a few words here and there, enough to see that they are the records of petty local crimes over which the Lord of the Manor, as magistrate for the district, would sit in judgement.

When Chris found the books and showed them to me we were both so intrigued that we turned detective in order to find the elusive 'Owby cum Thyrne'. It was not on any map that we could see, certainly not anywhere near Felbrigg. However, researches eventually led us to the watery flatlands of the Norfolk Broads, where there is a small but thriving community at secluded Thurne, its staithe crowded with boats in the summer, and with its restored water-pump on view. Nearby, one single small signpost points the way to 'Obi', which now consists of just one farm. We were thrilled to discover it and solve the mystery of 'Owby cum Thyrne'.

Perhaps the most interesting of the books is the oldest of the set: it dates from *the twenty-seventh year of the reign of Elizabeth*—Elizabeth I, of course, i.e. 1585. Not only that, but its parchment cover, which is probably even older, is made from an apprentice's indenture.

Chris put on a pair of white cotton gloves to protect the books as he displayed them for the interest of our transatlantic visitors. Such ancient manuscripts astounded the judges, lawyers and their wives. Fascinating! Wonderful! Where did they come from? Chris explained that he found them while sorting out old cupboards; they were stored in a tin box. The visitors found this even more amazing. How, they asked, was it possible to find such things just lying around at the back of cupboards?

The court books, and later a display of some of the other treasures from the Library, sent these particular visitors away delighted.

## Meanwhile . . .

As the main holiday season waned, Robert took the chance to have a week's break at his cottage. Meanwhile the work of the Hall went on, with open days as usual, workmen and deliveries, and no apparent decrease in visitor numbers.

In the autumn we usually hold our second special 'Garden Open' day in aid of the National Gardens' Scheme, repeating the procedure as in the summer. In September the colchicums in the garden are a sight worth seeing, great swathes of violets and mauves painted behind the dark green of box hedges. Felbrigg possesses the finest collection of colchicums in the country. And please, don't call them autumn crocuses, not where our gardeners can hear.

Regional office contacted us to say that another property, which was preparing to open more of its rooms to the public, needed an extra bed to complete its display. Borrowing of furniture between properties often has to be done in cases of deficiency, though it is our boast that all of Felbrigg's furniture and contents belong here, having been gathered over the years by succeeding generations of owners. Nothing has been added from elsewhere. In fact, we have much more than we can easily display in the main show rooms. So we were happy to let one bed go; it gave us more space in our crowded attics.

Chris spent several hours in the attics one morning with the historic buildings representative, showing him what beds were available and helping him decide which one might go best in the room for which it was needed. They finally settled on an unusual single four-poster, the twin to the charming bed which we have on display in our Chinese Bedroom. Chris moved it down from the attics and stored it somewhere more accessible, ready for collection.

Every time it rained, we continued to have problems with the leaking roof. Builders seemed to be in regularly trying to fix it, if only temporarily. The trouble would not finally be solved until the roof was releaded during our second winter at Felbrigg.

Another water problem began to show itself in the gents' lavatories, where the blockage in the drainpipe continued to recur. Chris tried all sorts of remedies, but it was becoming clear that this job too could only be properly remedied by major plumbing work which couldn't be attempted until after the end of the season—it would cause too much inconvenience! So in the meantime Chris had to keep checking and clearing the pipe as best he could.

The resurfacing of the estate roads also complicated life. On several days when we were open to the public, the tarmac-laying gang rapidly spread hot tar along the drive, followed by a thick layer of sharp chippings, with the result that many of our visitors complained bitterly about tar on shoes, on tyres, flying chippings, scratched paintwork, bicycle punctures . . . equally as annoying was the tar walked on to our floors and druggets, and the constant scatter of small sticky stones unavoidably brought in on visitors' shoes. The stones could be picked up; the tar was less easily dispersed.

We wondered what organising genius had arranged for the resurfacing to be done during the season.

A problem which pertains all year round concerns the parking of cars. To keep the approach to the house more attractive, and for the benefit of photographers, we try to ensure that the front courtyard is kept clear of vehicles. Our car park is ample, though it's about a hundred yards from the Hall; however, the exit from the gardens leads directly to the car park, so the distance need be walked only once. We do of course allow infirm or disabled passengers to be dropped at the door, and in the case of disabled *drivers* we make an exception—they may leave their cars in the front courtyard since, presumably, they will not be able to go round the gardens. Notices to this effect are displayed at the entry to the car park.

Nevertheless, disabled visitors frequently choose to leave their vehicles on the park rather than spoil the front of the house for everyone else. We see them approaching with crutches, walking frames, or in wheelchairs; their appreciation of our efforts to present the house in the most aesthetic way is very warming.

Other drivers occasionally leave their cars near gates, which may hamper the farmer and his workers. Also, some gates provide the only means of access for a wide vehicle such as a fire engine, which in an emergency could not get through if the gate were blocked. However many signs and notices we erect, someone will fail to see them. Mansion staff make many extra journeys to and fro during the season, trying to keep the ways clear.

Controlling the parking of vehicles is yet another area of the job that can be mined with difficulties.

## The New Flower-Arranger

Occasionally Gill, our flower-arranger, will for various reasons be unable to perform her miracle; she may go away for a few days, or be unwell. At first Eve filled in as deputy flower-arranger, but her job kept her away from Felbrigg so much that it became difficult for her to fulfil the commitment. This was one job I *couldn't* do, and certainly not for public viewing. I would help with the fetching and carrying, but Constance Spry I am not. We

The new flower-arranger

considered asking one of our lady room wardens to help out, but the difficulties of where she might work, the problems of getting water and the time involved in training her for a very occasional task seemed out of proportion. So in default of anyone else to do it, Chris took on that chore too.

To help out, Ted the head gardener kindly volunteered to select and cut the flowers; he left a huge bucketful of chrysanthemums, dahlias and foliage by the back door. Chris transferred them to the butler's pantry, which was the most convenient place for him to work, though it doesn't have a sink and so vases had to be emptied in, and fresh water fetched from, the restaurant kitchen. Our flat was too far away; using it would have involved a long trek with every vase and there just wasn't the time. But the job was done, one way or another.

People noticed that a new hand had arranged the floral displays. In the main they were complimentary, though one or two eyebrows lifted at the notion of a *man* doing such a job.

## Acorn Camps

Towards the end of September, the base camp was in use again, this time to accommodate a group of National Trust volunteers. These 'Acorn Camps' are held from time to time throughout the year when members gather over long weekends to help with labour-intensive work and 'megatasks' around our park and gardens, or those of other properties nearby. They might clear unruly rhododendron growth, build fences and walkways, or strengthen steps in woodland paths. After the disastrous hurricane in October 1987, when we lost three thousand trees, a group of YNT volunteers spent several weekends at Felbrigg gathering up wood debris and burning it on closely-tended fires. More recently, they have been delighted to be invited to help *inside* the house; they have acted as stewards for concerts, moved hundreds of books, and spent a morning happily engaged on the filthy task of cleaning out the cellars.

These young people, besides being of enormous help to the Trust, derive personal satisfaction from their hard work and from the social contacts they make. Evening at an Acorn Camp can be very convivial, as we know—they sometimes invite house staff to join them.

## Fire Practice

Another autumn evening was occupied with a Fire Practice—a dummy run for the brigade, whose engines were called out as if there were an emergency. When they set out, the men had no idea where they were heading (though of course their chief did; he had organised it with the Hall beforehand).

The tenders arrived at the Hall and the men went into their routine as if there really was a fire. They had to find the hydrants and fix their hoses while ladders were erected to reach the roof. Up they went to the dizzy heights of the leaded bays, from where they "made water" as they termed it, great arcs spraying from the roof to send their libations into the gravel courtyard far below. Unless there is a real emergency, fierce jets of water might cause damage to the slates, so in such practices the hoses will be directed away from the roof.

Later, having changed out of their waterproofs and helmets, the men walked through the house under the watchful eyes of Robert and Chris, in order to familiarise themselves with its layout in case of need. Such practices are usually held at least once a year. They make a spectacular change to the everyday routine and are of course vital to the safety of the Hall and everything in it.

## The Ketton Diaries

Many English houses have survived for centuries with their occupants periodically stuffing things away in the attics. When the same family occupies a house generation after generation, mementoes, broken toys and bric-à-brac pile up. How often does anyone tidy up an attic?

Since the Trust acquired Felbrigg it had been busy opening up the main rooms; only after we arrived was time found for the last corners and cupboards to be cleared out, so we had the privilege of finding many small treasures. The 'Owby cum Thyrne' court books were one example.

Another book which Chris found was apparently a rough record of rents and wages in 1926—or so it said on the cover —not very interesting except to someone studying historical minutiae, we thought. However, in the back of the book Chris discovered a sketchy journal. After long hours spent deciphering the handwriting, he realised that it had been written by John Ketton, the Norwich merchant who bought Felbrigg when it was sold by 'Mad' Windham in 1863.

No one had suspected this journal existed. As far as we can discover, even Mr Ketton-Cremer, the last owner of Felbrigg, did not know of it; he didn't mention it in his book *Felbrigg, the Story of a House*, though he quoted extensively from Mrs Ketton's diaries.

To our delight, the two journals coincided over a short period. According to Mrs Ketton, the butler, Norris, "accidentally locked up Margaret (one of the Ketton daughters) in the water closet where she passed the whole night suffering very much from cold" until she was discovered at 6 the next morning when one of the house-maids let her out. Mrs Ketton records the incident in vivid style; her husband says of the same day: "Weather very fine."

But there had been trouble with Norris before and one wonders how 'accidental' the locking-up was. Less than a month later, the butler was finally dismissed for "swearing at all the servants, and the family generally". Mrs Ketton was concerned to discover the silver plate, the pantry, and the beer cellar, "in a shocking state". The butler further aggravated her by having the effrontery to lodge with one of the woodsmen, from where he returned to the Hall on several occasions "before breakfast" to take away items which he considered belonged to him—his easy chair, and even some plants out of the greenhouse. Over several days Mrs Ketton records her dismay over the butler's behaviour, and having to encounter him about the estate. Her husband notes only "a violent quarrel between Butler (Norris) and Cook, quite a scene; gave Norris notice to leave the house that night, he went to the Woodsman's, an annoyance to me".

During the same period—April and May 1865—an entry by Mrs Ketton reads: "The Times gave the news that President Lincoln was assassinated. Sent to know how the dog was and heard it was quite well."

Mrs Ketton's diaries, interesting though they are, contain much trivia—who attended skating parties, who came to stay, and which neighbours lunched or dined; but then the life of many a Victorian matron revolved around social trivia. Her husband's journal is even more sketchy and has great gaps which he laments—evidently he had been persuaded that he ought to write a journal, but his heart wasn't in it. "Going on the same" is one inspired entry, followed by, "Ditto, Ditto, nothing to interrupt the usual course of things". He comments a great deal on the weather, noting the wind direction, and many entries read simply "Writing in the Morning, a walk afterwards," or "Writing in the Morning as usual, afternoon abt the Estate," or "Rather busy with letters, otherwise much as usual". He was a businessman and evidently had plenty of writing to do apart from his journal, but here and there fascinating details lie waiting—on April 30th 1865, he records: "Fairly busy with letters, the Railway (crossed out and amended to) Telegram Compy accept my offer for Larch Poles 500, this is an event for the Estate and I think will lead to increased value for Timber."

But Mr Ketton was often unwell. He frequently complains of feeling tired and ill: on the same days his wife often comments in her own diary: "John very cross and out of sorts." Mr Ketton's brief journal stops suddenly in June 1865. He died in 1872. However, after a blank page the journal continues in a more rounded (younger?) hand, covering nine days of an unrecorded month in 1874. Did Robert, his son and heir, make a brief stab at writing his own journal?

Such human details bring the Hall's owners vividly to life for us.

Holiday-makers in droves were still enjoying what was proving to be an Indian summer, and on our days off we too appreciated the fine weather as we travelled about the county exploring its contours and ancient sites as part of my research. Being in Norfolk had set me on the trail of the first known British queen —Boudicca (Boadicea).

Meanwhile at the Hall, despite the lovely autumn weather, we were thinking ahead and preparing for winter. Discussions were held on the correct wording of signs for the opening of our Christmas shop in November and December, when the main Hall would be closed. In the days that followed, the relevant signs were taken out of store and sent to be re-painted.

Joan was planning to offer Christmas lunches, which would need special advertising. She came to me with her ideas scribbled on a piece of paper and asked me if I would write a suitably inviting handbill, including all relevant information about the Christmas shop, opening days and times, and details of her proposed menu. The project was a new venture for me but I enjoy playing with words and between us we finalised a sheet to be duplicated on paper headed with FELBRIGG HALL and the Trust's acorn and oak leaf logo. As soon as they were ready, the handbills were left out for customers to pick up, and sent to various firms, hotels and other likely places.

Later, I discovered that the handbill was being used to advertise Christmas lunches in other properties, with the minimum of alterations to my wording. I was flattered that my first venture into advertising copy had been so successful—though maybe I should have sued for plagiarism.

## Darkening Days

Until the 1950s, when electricity reached the Hall, Felbrigg was equipped only with oil lamps. This may have been what saved the Hall from being requisitioned by the Army during the war. In the main rooms, to avoid damage to ceilings or walls, power was brought to plugs and switches set low, on or near the floors, so present-day illumination is provided mostly by standard and table lamps. An exception is the Drawing Room chandelier, which is wired for power and which sparkles with refracted rainbow colours when switched on. Lovely as it looks, though, it doesn't give much light.

As the days shortened into October, it was apparent that lights in the main show rooms would soon be a necessity. Some lamps had already been in use on afternoons when clouds darkened the sky, but in the final week of the season, after British Summer Time ended, our last hour of 'open' time would occur after nightfall. For safety's sake, the rooms must all be properly lit.

Anticipating the problem, Chris had for some weeks been checking all the lighting and searching the attics for extra lamps, rewiring some with the old-fashioned gold flex which he went to much trouble to find. And on our days off we had wandered the shops trying to find exactly the right shape and colour of very plain lampshade. Darker days would find the Hall equipped to counter them.

## Evening Occasion

Lights were essential not only for our regular afternoon visitors but for two very special evening events that were due. The first was an open evening for the benefit of one of our local National Trust Centres.

National Trust Centres are formed and run autonomously by National Trust members, with the aim of enabling them to share common interests. Activities include lectures, visits to properties, outings and other forms of social contact and entertainment. Members of the associations are encouraged to become actively involved in Trust work, and they raise funds for various Trust appeals, an area in which they are invaluable allies. Because they do such magnificent work for us, they are granted certain privileges—such as special openings on autumn evenings.

The group's organiser had asked Robert's permission for her members to make an evening tour of Felbrigg Hall, to see it lit up after dark and to have a buffet supper afterwards. Joan agreed to provide the supper; Peter said he would open the shop, so that members of the Centre could browse over choosing Christmas gifts in peace and quiet; and Chris of course would be responsible for the security and presentation of the Hall itself.

A Friday had been chosen for the event: with the house closed to the public on that day, Chris would have a little more time to perform all the necessary tasks such as preparing the Morning Room, where the group's members would gather as they arrived. At this time of year it would also be necessary to provide a place where coats could be left. Chris set out some chairs in the staircase hall for this purpose, and ensured that the cloakrooms were clean and ready. Most importantly, he made sure that all rooms had heaters on and lights in position.

As night fell, he did his rounds switching on the lights and then called me down to see the effect. How different the rooms looked when bathed in a mellow glow that lent a softer, more intimate atmosphere. From outside, with all the shutters thrown back and the blinds lifted, the house looked alive—a wonderful sight.

The association's advance party was due at 6. Kept busy to the last minute, Chris eventually came up to the flat at 5.45 for a bath and a change of clothes. He was becoming expert at the quick change from working garb to more formal wear and anticipated that fifteen minutes would be ample. However, as he was leaving a hasty bath, the doorbell rang—the *front* doorbell —the advance group was ten minutes early.

Grabbing a dressing gown, still dripping wet and without his glasses, he raced the half mile to the front door, fought with the rolled-back doormat, finally got the door open, and peered out myopically at the association's organising secretary and her companions. It was blowing a gale. He tried to preserve his modesty as the wind whipped at the edges of his dressing gown, while at the same time he apologised profusely for not being ready.

"No, no—we were early!" declared the organiser generously, trying to hide a grin. "You go and get dressed, we'll wait in the Morning Room."

Not forgetting to relock the door, Chris dashed back through

Chris welcoming early guests

the corridors towards the flat, facing a barrage of remarks from the restaurant ladies as he passed through their territory—they pulled his leg mercilessly for days afterwards. Five minutes later he was back, more decorously attired in suit, shirt and tie.

Despite the farcical aspect of its beginning, the evening was a great success. The visitors marvelled at the romantic aspect of the mansion with its lamps throwing pools of soft light across antique furniture and carpets while from the walls family portraits veiled in shadow looked down on the scene. Accompanied by Robert and Chris to answer questions and explain Felbrigg's history, the members of the association wandered through the main rooms, taking the usual visitor route along the ground floor, back to the main stairway and up to the Library; thence to the bedrooms, which with soft lamps gleaming looked as though they were waiting for welcome guests—perhaps Jane Austen or one of her heroines, someone suggested.

Later the party enjoyed a leisurely linger in the shop, followed by drinks and supper in the restaurant, and as they left they all expressed their appreciation of a really marvellous evening. It had been a pleasure for us, too. As Chris and I closed up the house, pulling down blinds, closing shutters, switching off heaters and lights, he felt that his long busy day had been well worth while. He always enjoys sharing his love of the Hall with other people, showing it at its best for them.

Such evenings are a small token of our appreciation for all the work the Centres do for the Trust. Without them, our job would be even more difficult.


The mirrors, pier table and wall brackets which had been on exhibition in the Victoria and Albert Museum for five months were all brought back now, checked for damage and put safely away until such time as Chris had an opportunity to restore them to their places, which proved not to be until after the house was closed for the season. At least they were safely home, none the worse for their sojourn in London.

Then regional office requested an inventory of all the pictures we have in the house—including those tucked away in the attics. This assignment would fill any spare moments Chris had during the next few weeks, though the job did bring its rewards: among other things, he found a John Sell Cotman drawing which no one had known was there.

This picture is some twelve inches by ten, a drawing of the church at Metton, a village which was once part of Felbrigg estate. It is evidence of Cotman's links with Felbrigg; he married Ann Miles, daughter of a local farmer, on 6th January 1809. The service took place in Felbrigg church and was conducted by the curate, John Lukin, brother of the squire, Admiral Lukin, who changed his name to Windham on inheriting the estate.

The finding of this drawing led Chris to yet another area of interest—the Norwich School of painters, of whom John Sell

Cotman was, next to John Crome, the leading light. As he delved into the subject, Chris discovered that Felbrigg possesses quite a few interesting paintings and drawings from the Norwich School. His investigations into the subject, hoping to verify details, are continuing.

A distressed visitor reported that someone going to the church had left a field gate open, allowing the entire herd of cattle to stray into the car park. Chris phoned the farmer and himself went to start moseying the herd back where they belonged. What with this and the summer-long involvement with newborn calves and their mothers, he was rapidly becoming an expert in the problems of a breeding herd of cattle.

A more contentious problem, also to do with the park, arose when we noticed that certain people—mainly teenagers—were suddenly starting to haunt the pasture early in a morning with their eyes on the ground, as if searching for something lost; occasionally they would swoop and pick something from the grass. Ted, our head gardener, told Chris this was an annual problem: because no chemicals were used on the pasture, a poisonous fungus called 'Liberty Cap' or more popularly 'magic mushroom', grew readily there every autumn. People in the know on the local drug scene came to pick these 'mushrooms', whose hallucinogenic properties can provide a dubious, dangerous thrill for anyone foolish enough to enjoy such a pastime; the magic mushrooms have, however, been known to kill. Nevertheless, the youngsters—some no more than ten or eleven years old—still came and searched amid the grass; when challenged, they chanted as if programmed, "Mushroom pie, mushroom pie," and how could we disprove this innocent claim?

In an effort to stop this practice, Robert sought help. But our land agent was powerless, it seemed. He knew no means of preventing people from picking mushrooms on National Trust property.

Not satisfied with this answer, Chris approached the local police for advice. But they too shrugged their shoulders—what did we expect them to do about it? They couldn't *prove* that the mushrooms were being used for illegal purposes.

Chris persisted. Surely we should be in the business of preventing drug abuse, not washing our hands when it was happening right in front of us? Besides, news of this unlovely harvest could redound to the detriment of the Trust.

It didn't happen at once, but in course of time the police agreed that he was right. In future, when he suspected anyone of gathering these mushrooms, he was to call the drug squad and they would send an officer, who would be interested to know who was involved in this unpleasant business. He would also be empowered to issue instructions that the culprits were not wanted on Trust property and if found again would be dealt with severely.

The police have kept their word; when the problem recurs they immediately respond to a call from Chris. Our volunteers too, apprised of the problem, have kept watch and reported any suspect activity they have witnessed. As a result, fewer 'mushroom pickers' disturb our misty autumn mornings. Hopefully, our vigilance may help to prevent some young person from falling victim to these lethal fungi.

## Samaritan Tendencies

Summoned from his lunch by an urgent message from the restaurant, Chris went down to find that a lady visitor was feeling unwell and her son, accompanying her, was rather anxious. The son said that his mother had a history of heart trouble; she would probably be all right if he could get her home but he didn't want to leave her in order to fetch his car, which was in the car park. Chris offered to bring the car up and even to drive them to a hospital, but the son didn't think that would be necessary. Once he had his mother safely in the car, he was sure he could manage. He handed over his car keys and Chris hurried across to the car park.

Only when he was in the driving seat did a low growl alert him to the fact that the passenger seat was occupied by a large dog, which evidently regarded him as having invaded its territory. Stern measures were called for. Unable to remember what

Barbara Woodhouse might have advised in such circumstances, Chris simply shouted, "Shut up!" and drove up to the Hall as quickly as he could. The dog, apparently shocked rigid by his tone of voice, sat stunned until it glimpsed its master approaching, when it whimpered pitifully in relief.

Such small acts of mercy are part of the day's diversions. Chris has lost count of the number of times he has helped people get into their cars when they've locked their keys in. He has recharged batteries, comforted lost children, aided the injured, searched for lost belongings—and frequently gone to great trouble to return such items: if visitors, or staff, are in trouble, he will always help, if only to the extent of lending moral support until more professional help arrives.

## The Dining Room

The public part of our lives is on view every time the Hall opens, but there is another facet to our relationship with Felbrigg—a personal, often emotional link which deepens with time. Everyone associated with the place has a favourite room, piece of furniture, or an episode in its history which they find of special appeal. Not surprisingly, these preferences are as varied as the people who own them.

Although I enjoy every aspect of the Hall and find something new to wonder at every time I walk round, some of the rooms are a little overpowering for my own personal taste: I could never sleep, for instance, in the Red Bedroom—the heavy striped wallpaper would keep me awake! And the Drawing Room and Cabinet, with their red walls, huge pictures and heavy gilt frames seem almost oppressive in their sumptuousness. On the other hand, both the Chinese Bedroom and the Rose Bedroom are charming.

But for me the favourite must be the Dining Room, for a variety of reasons.

The Dining Room retains its eighteenth-century décor—cool, elegant and not over-cluttered. It's the only room where, at present, visitors can wander freely without the channelling of red ropes, to study the bronzes or stare at the porcelain, or gaze out of any of three tall windows across the west lawn to the magnolia by the orangery, and to the park where the varied foliage of a wonderful bank of trees makes me wish I were an artist.

The polished dining table reflects a single glass candle-holder with crystal pendants; side tables hold glassware, and two sets of porcelain, one turquoise, one dark blue. The ceiling bears mouldings in which the four seasons are personified, with a great eagle set centrally, its talons clutched around a piece of wood. It was designed to support a chandelier, but the idea was never carried through.

On pale lilac walls the decorative plasterwork is picked out in white, forming garlanded frames for eight oval mirrors and for the family portraits above, several of which are also oval in shape. The frames are linked with fragile plaster chains, echoing the fetterlock to be seen everywhere in the family crest—in furniture, glassware, fireplace surrounds and especially in the stained glass windows in the Great Hall.

Among the portraits in the Dining Room are those of the first William Windham, and his wife, Katherine Ashe, and their oldest son Ashe Windham. Of all the characters down the centuries of Felbrigg history, Ashe is perhaps the one who attracts me most. His story is full of sadness.

Born in 1673, he was a boy of sixteen when his father died, so he came into his inheritance on gaining his majority five years later, in 1694. His portrait depicts an attractive young man wearing a flowing wig and blue coat—perhaps it's my imagination but I fancy the look in his eyes betrays a hint of the sorrow that was to be his lot in later life. While young he sired an illegitimate daughter, for whom he made careful provision, but despite family pressures he stubbornly held out against marriage for a long time.

And then at last, at the advanced age of thirty-five, Ashe fell deeply in love with a young girl named Hester Buckworth. She was of no particular fortune but evidently that did not matter to him; they became engaged. At the same time Ashe was persuaded to stand for Parliament. But towards the end of what proved a victorious political campaign, at what should have been a time of triumph, news came that his beloved Hester was dead, of the smallpox.

One can only guess at Ashe's feelings of grief. Perhaps he felt that nothing mattered any more. A little over a year later he pleased his mother by marrying Elizabeth Dobyns, a very rich heiress. She, however, proved to be a woman of perverse temperament, given to fits of melancholia and hysterics; she would probably be labelled spoiled and neurotic today. Within a year the marriage was foundering. After the birth of their son, William, in 1717 (when Ashe was forty-four), the couple separated.

To Ashe, his only son, coming so late into his life, was "more valuable than the riches of the Universe"; he vowed to his wife in a letter that "the care of him shall be the business of my life". But after William returned from a protracted Grand Tour in 1742 he formed some unsuitable liaisons that angered his father and caused an estrangement between them. During the final years of Ashe's life they hardly ever met. He died in 1749, a sad and lonely old man.

A portrait of his one real love, Hester Buckworth, hangs at the foot of the stairs, and his wife may be represented in one of the portraits in the Great Hall, though no one is entirely sure.

## The Regional Committee Dinner

The Dining Room, where Ashe Windham gazes down so soulfully, was to be the venue for that autumn's most important occasion —the regional committee dinner. It was a prestigious event and both Robert and Chris were anxious to make sure it went well.

The regional committee is a watchdog body which serves as a sounding board and means of liaison among staff and the public. Its members are deeply interested in the work of the National Trust; they are drawn from all walks of life. Among those expected at the coming dinner were Lords Lieutenant and other important personages from across East Anglia, along with the regional director who would act as host for the occasion.

The date coincided unhappily with a few personal worries for us: I had to go into hospital for an operation and was not discharged until the morning of the day of the dinner—fetched by my parents, who were staying with us in order to reassure themselves of my wellbeing. And as if that were not enough, Kevin was sent home sick from the nurses' home. So the small flat was crowded, two of us being semi-invalid. Such things, as they say, are sent to try us. But personal traumas were only the beginning. . . .

The dinner had been organised for a Tuesday evening—an 'open' day—so the Dining Room couldn't begin to be prepared until the day's visitors had gone and the house was closed, at 6 p.m. However, certain other preparations could be completed ahead of time and for several days Chris had been systematically polishing the silver tableware and glassware which belong to the house. The huge silver candelabra, the salt cellars and spoons, the knives and forks, the crystal goblets . . . all would be used to dress the dining table.

On the day of the dinner he took out the polished silver and glass, and left them ready in the butler's pantry, along with the thick baize cloth which would protect the surface of the table. The butler's pantry lies midway on the lengthy route between Dining Room and kitchen. It is a practical workroom used mainly by the cleaners and not on view to the public. This evening it was to provide a useful staging post for those who were serving the meal.

The usual 'open' day routine was carried out, room wardens on duty and shop and restaurant busy with a fair number of visitors despite overcast skies and the gloom of a late October afternoon. Well before 6 o'clock the house was empty, so Chris closed up promptly. Having said goodbye to the room wardens and locked the doors, he immediately started to prepare for the evening's function, clearing the display glassware from the vast Dining Room table, which can seat sixteen with room to spare.

The regional committee members were expected at 8, to dine at 8.30. Just under two hours to go.

Joan and her assistants sprang into action, too, as soon as the last customer had left the tea-room. They spread the baize cloth in the Dining Room, smoothing it down before laying starched white tablecloths and bringing out the gleaming silver and glassware, while Chris organised an extra heater and another lamp or two. Meanwhile in the kitchen the food was being prepared, the roast of beef beginning to send delicious aromas along the corridor. All was going to plan.

"All we need now is a power cut," Chris said.

The gods must have heard him. Only seconds later, with a silent thud, the lights went out.

Fortunately torches were kept not far away and by now Chris knew the Hall well enough to move around in the utter blackness which obtains here at night. The ladies continued to lay the table by torchlight while he went to beam his little ray into the appropriate cupboard where the electricity junction boxes are situated. Was the problem in the mains, or in our own system? As he moved through the house he glimpsed lights shining from tenants' windows across the courtyard, so it couldn't be the mains.

He checked the fuse boxes. We have two separate phases for our power; only one had gone, which was the good news. The bad news was that the failure was in the very phase whose loss could spell disaster, that night of all nights—it brought power to the main downstairs rooms, the butler's pantry and—wouldn't you know?—the kitchens. Not only had the lights gone, but the heaters and cookers were no longer functional: the rooms would rapidly grow chill; the part-cooked food would soon start to cool, the preparations had come to a halt . . . PANIC STATIONS!

Chris phoned the electricity board, impressing urgency upon them, then swiftly moved through the Hall establishing the position of the nearest available socket still supplied with power. Having found it, he ran extension cables to an area from where the dinner could still be operated, mainly by means of the restaurant's heated trolley, which suddenly became Joan's most invaluable asset.

She and her staff, meanwhile, were concerned with rescuing the food from imminent disaster. Since power was on in some of the tenants' apartments, some items from the menu were rushed across the grass courtyard and distributed among various cookers. Gill, who does the flowers, agreed to play hostess to the vegetables; another lady, with a solid fuel cooker, lent an oven to the enormous baron of beef; and the Yorkshire pudding pans and batter came up to our flat ready to go into our oven at the appropriate moment.

Downstairs, an electricity board engineer had arrived. Chris took him into pitch-dark woods and showed him the pole where the transformer was situated. One look told the man it was a job he could not, under rules of safety, handle alone: he had to radio for assistance, which meant a further delay. Great!

Returning to the Hall, Chris was obliged to accept the probability that the power might not be restored in time. Some means of continuing with the regional committee dinner had to be found, despite the odds. He could keep doors closed to preserve what heat there was, but lighting was the main problem—torchlight was hardly adequate for a formal dinner. Candles were the obvious answer, though in most circumstances naked flames are directly contrary to Trust policy because of the risk of fire.

Meanwhile Robert had contacted the regional director and informed him of the emergency, asking if we ought to cancel the dinner. But that was out of the question; the regional director pointed out that by now (past 7 o'clock) the chairman and half the committee would be *en route*; some of them were coming from neighbouring counties. Candles it would have to be—with appropriate safety precautions, of course.

Of course. Safety is always a priority. Chris hurriedly placed fire extinguishers at strategic points and brought out all the brass candlesticks and candelabra he could find, supplying them with candles from store. As the flames sprang to life, flickering light and shifting shadows evoked the past, creating a spine-tingling ambience in the rather ponderous, early Victorian décor of the Great Hall where the guests would be received.

As 8 o'clock approached, Robert appeared, ready dressed to greet the first VIP arrivals. Joan brought in trays of sherry and reported that the food at its various venues was doing fine. Despite difficulties, it looked as though everything would come together on time.

Realising that he was still in his afternoon clothes, Chris sent up to the flat for his suit and clean shirt. There was no time for anything but a quick change in the Morning Room. He had barely finished when a car drew up in the darkened courtyard and he went to meet the car's occupants and light their way into the Great Hall—by means of a three-branched candelabrum.

He had never used a candelabrum in such a way before. Unlike a torch, which one holds in front, candles have to be held to one side and a little behind the line of sight, otherwise the light dazzles the porter. Candles aloft, he glimpsed his reflection in

Chris had never used a candelabrum in such a way before

the glass fire doors of the lobby—he could have auditioned for the part of hunch-backed 'Igor' in a Dracula movie.

Luckily the first arrivals were the regional director and the chairman of the regional committee, both familiar friends of Felbrigg, but other members of the committee were not far behind. Chris informed them of the problems with the electricity but assured them that the only hardship they might suffer was from lack of heat; everything else was well in hand. The Dunkirk spirit prevailed—hot food and generous supplies of wine would help keep them warm, they joked. They exclaimed in delight over the glamorising effects of candlelight as they congregated convivially with their sherry in the Great Hall, while Chris remained by the front door to light the others in.

An element of farce was introduced when, out of the darkness across the courtyard, Chris heard voices, and glimpsed a spectral figure garbed in flowing, light-coloured attire.

"Hello? Who's that?" he called.

"It's only me!" floated the voice of one of our lady room wardens. She said that she had heard how marvellous the Hall could look when lit up at night, so she had made a special trip just to see it. A delightful, well-travelled lady who likes to wear the costume of countries she has visited, she was dressed that evening in her white cotton East Indian outfit, trousers and floaty top which gleamed palely in the night and added a bizarre touch to an already crazy evening. Chris had visions of her drifting past the windows, reviving tales of ghosts at Felbrigg, as the regional committee dined.

However, her presence proved fortuitous because her arrival had coincided with that of the extra men from the electricity board and, learning the situation, she kindly showed them the way to the stable yard, where Chris met them and took them into the woods.

Thanks to quick thinking and inspired team-work, the dinner was a tremendous success. Chris remained on duty in the wings, standing by for any further crisis, though fortunately our store of crises was empty for the moment. As the members of the regional committee departed around midnight, they declared that it had been a wonderful evening—seeing the Hall in such an evocative, romantic atmosphere, and dining by candlelight, had been an unexpected bonus.

When British Summer Time ends, the clocks are put back. In most houses this is a fairly simple task: not so at Felbrigg. The Hall possesses many different clocks, from tiny French enamelled beauties to the great stately long-case "grandfathers", all have their own individual characteristics and foibles, so each one must be handled in a special way. Chris usually puts them back an hour simply by stopping them, and since it takes him about an hour to go round every one by the time he has finished it's time to start up the first ones again. He tries to keep all the clocks working and accurate—something our visitors often comment upon with pleasure. Their ticking seems like the heartbeat of each room, bringing it to life, and their various chimes ring melodically along hallways and corridors.

But with the end of BST, of course, the nights came earlier; for the final week of the season darkness fell well before the house closed. The rooms were cold despite blow heaters and some of our volunteers were not keen on going home in the dark. Besides, the number of visitors was down to a trickle now. There was a sense of approaching quietude, a readiness for slumber, a winding down towards the last day of the season. . . .

Or so it may have appeared to some. For house staff all systems remained at 'go'.

Autumn is the time when the National Trust holds training courses. Chris attended one during the last week of our first season, a one-day course intended "to help familiarise new members of staff with the requirements of the Trust"—assuming the past year hadn't been demonstration enough. On Friday of that week we held another concert, followed by the usual candle-lit supper, and on the Saturday morning we had another 'special opening' for another National Trust Centre. These visitors were guided through the house by Chris and round the gardens by

Robert before they all came back for a lunch which Joan had prepared.

The last Sunday in October, or the first Sunday in November, is usually the last day of opening. It can be relatively busy; people seem keen to take one last look at the rooms before the house is 'put to bed' for the winter. But it's dark, and often freezing cold, by the time the room wardens take their final leave and they are not sorry to be going home, looking forward to a break during the darkest months.

"What do you do now?" one of them inevitably asks. "Put your feet up until March, I expect."

Why does this impression persist so stubbornly, even among those who ought to know better?

## 6

# Winter Again—The Christmas Opening Season

### *Winding Down*

After the house has closed to the public, one of the first tasks is to take in signs which are now misleading and which will be repainted for next year; other signs go out—signs relevant to the Christmas opening season.

During the Christmas period—from now until Christmas Eve —the shop and restaurant are open from 11 a.m. until 4 p.m. on the same days as during the season, the difference being the earlier hours and the fact that the Hall itself is no longer on view. However, that doesn't mean that the Hall is quiet, or that house staff can relax: the cleaners will be busy, needing help and supervision; and necessary repair, renovation and maintenance jobs can at last be started on, so workmen will be in and out once more, with all the complications that can entail when shoppers and lunchers still need access to the cloakrooms.

Once the Hall closes to visitors, the cleaners start to prepare the main rooms for a period of hibernation. Ropes and stanchions which have marked the visitor route are put away; curtains are loosened from their bands, shaken out and allowed to hang, to air out the creases. The cleaners remove all small items from the main rooms: glassware, china and porcelain, clocks etc. are wrapped in acid-free paper to protect them from harm, then they are stored away until spring. As each room is cleared, heavy dust sheets are fetched out to drape the furniture.

The houseman will be available to help cover the largest items such as wardrobes and beds. This calls for the use of step-ladders; furniture may also have delicate wood carving which must be unscrewed or otherwise protected. Putting the rooms to bed, under cover for the winter, takes at least two weeks to complete.

## Dust Covers

Heavy linen dust sheets can be difficult to handle and they make it awkward to move furniture about as cleaning progresses, not to mention the enormous weight involved when three or four sheets are needed to cover, for instance, the tester of a four-poster bed, which may not have been designed to support such a load. At Felbrigg we have been fortunate to secure the help of a group of ladies, members of a Fine Arts society, who for two or three winters past have been busy making case covers—individual covers shaped to each piece of furniture, in a very light cotton material.

During the winter, as often as they can, the ladies bring their own sewing machines and settle down at trestle tables set up for them in the Morning Room. They are applying a different colour bias binding for each room—red for the Cabinet, dark blue for the Drawing Room. . . .Those two rooms are now supplied with sets of covers; the rest are in the making, or for the future. It's an enormous undertaking that will probably take several more years to complete but when the covers are finally finished they will be a terrific asset to the house.

The sewing ladies all give their work voluntarily and cheerfully. They are a merry addition to our winter scene.

## The Visitation

Soon after the end of the main season, the annual 'Visitation' meeting is held. At this meeting the season past and the season to come are reviewed by departmental heads—administrator, houseman, shop manager, restaurant manageress, head gardener and head woodsman—together with members of the regional office support staff, under the chairmanship of the regional director. Everyone on the list of staff at the property is invited to share coffee with the rest—the cleaners, the restaurant and shop helpers, assistant gardeners and woodsmen, the Manpower Services Commission team which is currently rebuilding the estate wall—plus resident wives, who may not appear on the pay roll but are still a vital part of the team. However, since attendance at coffee is not compulsory some shyer individuals may avoid the occasion, not being keen on 'meetings' in any form.

At the meeting proper, any large-scale plans and any need for further changes are discussed. The new restaurant having proved an outstanding success, our next most urgent need was the provision of lavatories outside the confines of the Hall, to eliminate the need for visitors constantly to penetrate the depths of the house. This was in hand, we were assured. (In the event, it took four years; the new loos are being completed even as I write.)

The Visitation meeting lasted through lunch in the restaurant and into the afternoon. When eventually it ended, Chris continued with his immediate end-of-season tasks such as clearing the reception desk, storing guide books away, clearing the recruiters' table and helping to set up staging and tables so that the shop could spread from its usual quarters. Peter and his wife were busy arranging their Christmas stock to spill enticingly along the corridors, ready to welcome shoppers as they entered by the Rose Garden door.

In our second year, as an experiment, shoppers came in at the main door and were allowed to visit the Great Hall and the Morning Room, which was decked out for an old-fashioned Christmas. A huge tree was set up and trimmed with candles and home-made decorations, and toys brought from the attics were laid out at its foot—a Noah's ark, complete with a set of hand-carved animals, two by two; a large model taxi; a well-loved lion (which still growls if asked); and a teddy bear loaned by Eve. There were festoons and garlands along the mantelpiece, from where stockings hung, and fruit and nuts on a table, along with hand-made cardboard drums and trumpets, pretend parcels, baubles and berries, holly and ivy fresh from the gardens. . . .

Sadly, this attraction endured for only one season; opening the two large show rooms meant having to keep those rooms well heated, plus recruiting two volunteers every day to keep an eye on security, and most of all it delayed the essential winter conservation work without bringing any tangible benefits. Even so, those of us—and our visitors—who saw it will always remember how enchanting the Morning Room looked for those few weeks.

## Into Hibernation?

When the house is at last all settled under its dust sheets, the cleaners start on the job which they confess they dislike most of all—clearing a year's dust, cobwebs, dead flies and bat-droppings from the warren of cold, gloomy, rummage-filled rooms which comprise our attics. It's an unpleasant, dirty job which they hope to complete before the weather turns too cold—there are no electrical points for heaters and lights in the attics. The ladies work in murky twilight, well-wrapped in body-warmers, several sweaters, scarves, hats and gloves. It will take at least a fortnight to dust and sweep all twelve rooms and the long landings under sloping eaves.

Next, having finished the attics, the ladies turn their attention to the base camp, which is given a thorough cleaning before its water is turned off and the system drained; then the base camp too is closed up for the winter. The houseman will, as always, help with any heavy jobs, or in any way he may be needed.

One year Chris decided to strip all the loose covers from the base camp armchairs; they were pretty grubby and looked as though they hadn't been washed for years. He brought them to me and asked if our washing machine could cope with the job, to save the Trust the cost of dry cleaning. Four machine loads later, sixteen chair covers festooned our bathroom, landings and stair well—lacking a garden, I had nowhere else to hang them. They were there for days before they were properly dry. But they did look better, especially after I had mended all the torn seams and darned the holes. The base camp gets a lot of heavy wear during the season.

The furniture expert returned to advise on the refixing of the Rococo mirrors and other furnishings which had been on exhibition in London. He and Chris unpacked the items from their crates and with great care replaced them in the appropriate rooms. The tiny polystyrene beads which had protected them in transit were light as air and the least breath caused them to drift in clouds. For several years the cleaners would continue to find odd remnants of these white beads trapped in cobwebs or caught in inaccessible corners.

Throughout the winter, the furniture expert will be a fairly regular visitor as he returns pieces he has restored and takes away others for treatment.

A three-day course on Housekeeping gave Chris a short break from his regular duties. It was held at a property in Devon, to where he drove from Norfolk. On his way back, he collected our elder son from Bristol and took him—and his belongings—to new quarters at Nottingham; Andrew was changing universities again, having completed an M.Sc. at Bristol he was going on to do a Ph.D. Lucky his father was going to be in the area to help out!

The morning after Chris returned, he had an early meeting with the building manager from regional office to discuss what work needed to be done that winter, beginning with the urgent attention to the blockage in the gents' washbasins. Builders started to tackle the problem on the next 'closed' day for the Christmas shop but the job was more complicated than anticipated and needed longer than a day to complete. The work —and cleaning up after the workmen—had to be timed to cause the least possible disruption and hindrance to visitors.

Needing to get at the drains, the men were in and out through a side door, bringing in mud and muck which they inevitably tramped down the corridor and into the gents'. Chris seemed to be constantly scrubbing the floors clean and setting heaters to dry the flagstones ready for the next influx of shop and restaurant visitors.

At the same time, other workmen were busy in the Drawing Room, where the glazing bars on one of the huge windows had been found to be rotting. The window had to be removed. The problem, as the workmen discovered, was how to accomplish this seemingly impossible feat; the window appeared to be solidly fixed, with no apparent means of opening it. When Chris suggested that logically there must be some way of opening it, the builders shook their heads in mystification.

Had they thought of trying to push it straight up—a window in the Morning Room opens this way? The builders had their doubts but, when eventually they agreed to give the theory a try, to their surprise the window slid up easily, into a cavity in the wall; it was a sash window, cunningly worked by immense weights hidden in the frame. Once opened, it was a relatively simple matter to ease it free, angle its bottom end into the room and carefully manoeuvre it outside. Simple, that is, taking into account the care needed not to damage interior walls and paintings.

The window was so unusual that it drew a deal of interest from everyone involved. One of the plumbers who was working on the gents' lavatory strolled into the Drawing Room to see what his mates were up to. He walked right across the drugget *and* the precious carpet, with boots caked with wet mud, plaster, cement. . . .

## The Armada Chest

Our buildings' advisers had recognised a need to strengthen ceilings in the 'lock-up' area. This warren of store rooms, on two floors at the end of a wing, had been used for many different purposes over the years. Part of it was once a game parlour; great hooks still protrude from its old ceiling beams. There was also, according to some old plans, a gun room, a knife room and a strong room—the 'lock-up' itself. Now, some areas provide a store for heavy and dirty lumber, another is the houseman's workshop, and yet another holds freezers and other storage for the restaurant.

Before work on the ceilings could begin, Chris had to clear most of the rooms. But, yet again, hard work brought its reward when he came across an old chest, mouldering away beneath piles of rubbish. To his delight it turned out to be an Armada chest (so-called, though it has nothing to do with the Spanish Armada).

As far as we can discover, such chests probably originated in Germany during the mid-eighteenth century. Ours has a wonderful multiple lock with seven bolts worked from a central keyhole, which is cleverly hidden behind an escutcheon. And unlike most such chests, which are often painted a dull brown or black, ours has its original painting—small figures and boats can be made out against a green background. The chest was in terrible condition when Chris found it, the bottom beginning to rust; in a short while it would have collapsed under its own weight. Now, at least, it has been placed clear of further damp and its condition is stabilised. Perhaps one day the time, and the funds, will be found to have it properly restored and put on show.

On a free weekend, we took a walk around the lake—a good hour or more's hike through fields and marshy hollows, but always an invigorating experience. The countryside, fields and woods are beautiful at any time of year, even in November with bare branches spread against mournful skies, and the ground soggy underfoot, squelching deep in dead leaves. There are ducks and geese on the lake, squirrels to spy, a woodpecker hammering and possibly a kingfisher to flash a glimpse of bright blue. Birds wheel and flow across the pasture—Brent geese, Canada geese, different gulls, rooks, crows; white birds, black birds, all swooping and calling in flocks.

But despite such peaceful moments, the work went on. One lunchtime an unexpected rush caught the restaurant staff short-handed and Chris, passing through, asked what he could do to help. He was set to cutting up salad vegetables, while a call came up for me to help clear tables. Even our land agent, present for a meeting with Robert, lent a hand at the height of the rush. Between us, we rode the waves and kept our visitors happy.

Towards the end of the month another 'Housekeeping Day' —a reiteration of the Trust's policy on cleaning, in readiness for the coming winter's onslaught—was to be held at another property nearby. Chris and all four cleaners were expected to attend, so he spent the previous evening washing kitchen floors, cleaning loos, vacuum-cleaning shop and corridors. . . . "Washday hands—washerwoman's knees!" was his rueful comment.

During several relatively quiet days, he managed to complete the picture inventory wanted by the historic buildings representative. At other moments he had small maintenance tasks to attend to, the usual opening up and closing down procedures, seeing to workmen and other visitors—and if someone arrived wanting to join the Trust as a member he would act as recruiter, too.

## The Roof

At 10 o'clock one bleak and misty morning, people started gathering for an important meeting concerning the re-leading of the roof—this major project was about to start. Relevant personnel from regional office arrived, then the architects, and representatives of roofing contractors and scaffolding firms; Robert and Chris made up the complement. Long discussions took place concerning ways and means of accomplishing the job.

The roof is a broad area of angular hills and peaks formed by oak timbers under a combination of graded Collyweston slates, with leaded gulleys and flats. The oldest parts of it date from Jacobean times. The Collywestons' grey, softly lichened appearance is enhanced by the skill with which the slates have been placed, large ones at the bottom of each slope, shading through several sizes to the small ones at the apex; they are a tribute to the slater's craft.

The roof was last releaded just over a century ago. On one area we discovered some markings, presumably left by the workmen who performed the task. A shoe-print and a hand-print were pricked out in outline, alongside the name "T. Rudd", and the initials "J.M.A.", and "W.H.F.", with the dates "1880" and "1878". This historic piece of lead was carefully removed and, when the renovations were complete, was welded on to an area of the re-leaded roof, so it is preserved.

As discussions on the project continued it became apparent that the renovation would involve the removal of the entire central area of the roof and the erection of fresh timbers and a new 'lantern'—the great skylight which illuminates the main staircase hall. A vast network of scaffolding would be needed, both outside and inside the house, including the full height of the staircase hall. The contents of the hall would need to be protected, chairs and ornaments moved right out of the way, portraits taken down (a task which was to prove extremely difficult as some of the pictures hang high over the stairs well out of reach except with the aid of scaffolding and several people to help). One enormous portrait, too large to risk moving, would have to be enclosed in a specially-made box. Also, during the course of the work parts of the attics would, for a time, be open to the elements, though boarding and tarpaulins would be used. The workmen would need huts to shelter in, and with scaffolding around the house extra security measures would be necessary. There were a hundred and one things to be considered.

The meeting moved from the office, through various areas of the Hall and out into the gardens as they discussed all possibilities. So much talking made them all thirsty; they needed a break for coffee. It being a 'closed' day, with the restaurant not functioning, they all came up to our flat.

Obviously the re-leading was going to take several months, and that over the winter when bad weather might cause extra delays. We only hoped they would begin pretty soon, otherwise the roof might not be finished by the time we wanted to open again in the spring.

## Of Ghosts and Gremlins

People often ask if Felbrigg is haunted. Certainly with the onset of long dark nights, of hoar frosts and howling gales, it would be easy to believe so. The wind wails in the chimneys; the old house begins to creak and groan. Closed shutters allow no chink of moonlight or starglow to lighten absolute blackness. Nor are there any electric lights that can flick off the dark at the touch of a switch. Called out by some emergency after dark, resident house staff move about with only the aid of torches, through shrouded rooms where shadows loom large. Under such conditions, imagination may conjure all kinds of demons.

There are, inevitably, a few ghost stories connected with the Hall, but whether they are true or not is a question of faith. The most famous incident concerned a staff member of the National Trust, working at Felbrigg soon after the Trust had acquired it. A level-headed, sober and trustworthy witness—so we are assured—he was working alone in the Library when he looked up and saw the form of a man sitting in one of the green leather chairs. As so often happens in such tales, the witness thought nothing of this until he glanced up again and the apparition had vanished. From its clothes and general appearance, the 'ghost' was thought to be William Windham III.

We have never met the gentleman who is reputed to have seen this ghost. Details of the story alter depending on whom one talks to, but it's a favourite spine-chiller among some of our guides, who swear that "books have been opened at night"—sure evidence that Windham III returns to read from his collection. However, we ourselves have never known this to happen since we have been here.

There are other tales, too ill-evidenced to repeat in detail, including one account of a 'psychic' visitor who claimed that she could see maidservants rushing from one of the buildings at the rear of the Hall, where there was a fire. So far, we can discover no evidence of there having been such a fire.

I try to retain an open mind on the subject; I find it fascinating and would love to have experience that would convince me such tales are true. Chris, on the other hand, is a total sceptic who believes it is all in the mind of the beholder.

But even he has to report one or two incidents. . . .

One winter night, walking through the bedrooms on some errand, he glimpsed a ghostly figure walking in the *opposite* direction. On another occasion, when he had just closed the Library shutters, leaving himself in total darkness, he was walking back across the room towards the door when he felt a hand on his shoulder. . . .

If he had been of a nervous disposition, he would probably have fled, and both of these incidents would by now have been added to the store of Felbrigg's ghost lore. Being a sceptic, however, he knew there had to be a rational explanation, so he retraced his steps to find it.

The 'ghostly figure' was in fact a reflection of his reflection, thrown between mirrors placed fortuitously just where one would reflect an image on to the other, thus relaying the image in reverse—which was why the figure appeared to be crossing the room in the opposite direction. And the 'hand on the

A 'ghostly hand' on the shoulder

shoulder' turned out to have been the wooden acorn weight on the end of the long cord of the Library blind; when Chris exactly repeated his movements it happened again—the cord caught on his shoulder as he moved away from the window, but since he was wearing a thick anorak he didn't feel it until he reached the middle of the room, when the acorn lightly tapped him as it slipped over his shoulder.

But then again, there was the incident after we moved into the administrator's flat, when early in the morning I discovered a door ajar—a door which is normally kept bolted, which links our flat with the main Hall, and whose opening *should* have set the alarms off. . . . Chris can explain it away. I'm not convinced.

Is Felbrigg haunted?

Who knows?

## Christmas is Coming . . .

On a 'closed' day at the end of November, Peter came in to begin putting up Christmas decorations in the shop. Later the same day, Joan and her husband arrived with the same intentions for the restaurant. Trees were decorated, crêpe paper laid, baubles and tinsel hung from walls and shelving. The Hall once more donned its festive face.

With Christmas only four weeks away, business in the shop increased and consequently the restaurant too was even busier. They served Christmas lunches every Sunday and were soon completely booked for these. The Christmas menu could also be served on weekdays by special arrangement, otherwise our usual hot dishes or selection of salads and snacks were available. Many people travelled long distances to enjoy their Christmas shopping and a leisurely lunch at Felbrigg Hall; our fame was spreading.

In the Hall itself, Chris and the cleaners worked hard to clear the 'lock-up' area for the builders who were coming to strengthen the ceilings, and when that was finally done the ladies turned their attention to the Library, where they began the long task of cleaning and examining all the books. That would keep them busy to the Christmas break and beyond.

However, their work in the Library was briefly interrupted by the need to clean and prepare the Morning Room for the final concert of the season—a Christmas concert which was to be held on a Sunday afternoon. All of the seats were sold for this special programme of Christmas music. Many of the concert-goers booked lunch beforehand; the restaurant was full. On that day, everyone available was again called on to help and the Hall came alive with evocative, seasonal music that filled us all with nostalgia and excitement.

The following week our quota of Christmas trees arrived, culled from the estate in various shapes and sizes to be laid out in the Rose Garden. Two big ones were chosen for use in the Hall; one in the corridor and one in the shop, when decorated and hung with lights they brought a real sense of approaching Christmas. The rest of the trees went on sale to customers who had been ringing up for days asking when they would be available.

Then the builders arrived to start strengthening the ceilings in the 'lock-up'. They started at 8.15 a.m., so Chris had to be on duty in time to open the house and let them in. The first thing they did was to erect scaffolding and remove a window so that they could easily dispose of bags of old plaster and rubbish which they would be bringing down by the ton. . . .

## Party Time

However, if the December work diary is just as full as any other month it does offer a few compensations: it is the time for parties and saying thank you to everyone who has helped during the year.

Our main staff party was to be held on a Friday evening, in the Morning Room, but expected to spill into corridors and restaurant when the buffet was served. Robert and Eve had sent out around a hundred invitations—to everyone who worked in or was connected with the house or the estate, and their partners, plus people from regional office.

To accommodate them all, Chris cleared much of the furniture from the Morning Room, leaving a few chairs, the odd table—and the piano, which was too large to leave the room and which anyway might be called into service later. The concert chairs were carried into the staircase hall where they would provide a place for coats, and the brass candlesticks were cleaned of old wax and polished again.

The restaurant too had to be partially cleared if it was to provide room for everyone. On the evening prior to the party, Chris and I moved half the tables and chairs into an adjacent corridor as overflow seating, and manhandled the long buffet table to a more suitable position. The restaurant staff were busy most of the next day preparing a wonderful buffet spread, but when the party began they were able for once to relax, leaving the serving to other help which Joan had drafted in for the evening.

The party was a happy occasion. It was good to see old friends returning, filling the house with their laughter and good-natured leg-pulling. As they arrived they were greeted at the door by Robert and Eve, and served with wine before they mingled in the Morning Room. Later, speeches were made and thanks expressed for all the hard work which had given us such a successful season. Later still, after we had eaten and the crowd thinned, someone struck up with carols on the piano and the evening ended in a sing-song. Warm with wine and friendship, the last few guests lingered and, to let Chris 'lock down' and feel free to have a drink himself, we invited the remaining revellers up to our flat, where we talked far into the night.

A few days later, the Trust held a wine and cheese party for tenant farmers and their wives—a quieter affair, but equally pleasurable and convivial. After it, the Morning Room was cleaned again, the concert chairs brought back and restacked. The cleaners continued in the Library. Work went on.

Jobs continued to pile up without respite: a shutter knob caused Chris hours of work because he had actually to *make* a replacement screw to fix it; scaffolding men spent most of a day on the roof assessing what had to be done and finding numerous problems that would complicate their task; the head housekeeper visited again; and a delivery of 115 bottles of wine had to be carried down to the cellar. . . .

Suddenly it was the last weekend before Christmas. On Saturday Robert set off for his cottage, where he would have a ten-day break over the holiday. It was our turn to remain on duty. With both our sons expected home this was no real hardship except that we should be unable to go out all together over the festive period—someone always has to house-sit in case of emergencies.

On Sunday the shop was busy, the restaurant working at capacity serving Christmas lunches. The same story was repeated on Monday, Christmas Eve—the restaurant was so crowded that Chris was again called in to help clear tables.

Also on Christmas Eve our sons arrived by train. Andrew came from Nottingham to Norwich where Kevin joined him and they both took the local diesel to Cromer, only three miles away from the Hall. I picked them up and brought them home, delighted by their presence about the flat. It was really beginning to feel like Christmas, with rustlings of paper, requests for sealing tape, "Haven't you left us any gift tags, Mum? Oh, typical!" and heavy rock music blaring from the second bedroom. I'd have preferred carols, but never mind, there was a good old Cecil B. de Mille movie on TV. With half an eye I admired the young Charlton Heston's physique as I baked pastry, while the boys were collecting gravel to weigh down the Christmas tree's bucket container, before they began to rediscover old friends from the trimmings box.

Chris and the rest of the staff hoped to end their working day as soon as possible after 4 o'clock—everyone in the house, including the boys and me, gathered in the restaurant for a Christmas drink at that hour. But fortune decreed a final frustration when the market gardener was delayed. He had been coming twice a week to replace flowering plants which were on sale in the shop and now he had to remove the remaining plants which had not been sold. It was past 4.30 when he eventually turned up, but how could we carp when he kindly presented Joan, and Peter's wife, and me, with plants as Christmas gifts? When he had gone, the staff departed, after which Chris finally closed down the house and came up to the flat to begin his own holiday break.

Christmas morning was a leisurely affair. We lazed around over coffee, opening our presents and listening to a recording of *The Messiah*. Towards 11 o'clock we got ready to go out—we had all been invited to have drinks with our neighbours, Gill the flower-lady and her husband, and most of our small community were there to share the occasion. Afterwards we returned to a light lunch and spent the afternoon lazily, in between whiles doing what was necessary for the traditional Christmas dinner, most of which I had prepared the previous day. By the time we finished dinner late that evening, we were all mellow enough to enjoy a game of Trivial Pursuit.

Boxing Day was equally laid back. We couldn't go far from the Hall—at least, Chris couldn't—but we did take a stroll in the gardens before returning to the warmth of the flat. On our way back, we encountered a family of four wandering in the private courtyard behind the Hall, looking for the lavatories. We were obliged to say that there were no lavatories available except perhaps in Cromer, where the nearest public toilets were, hopefully, open despite the holiday.

However, the two children seemed to be in such desperate need that we allowed them up to use the toilet in our flat.

After two blissfully quiet days, the siren call of work waiting to be done, so close at hand, proved too much for Chris. He spent most of the 27th doing accounts and other paperwork to complete the banking as soon as possible. During the following two days Peter came in to do his stock-taking, then after a quiet Sunday the world was back.

Carpet layers arrived first thing on Monday morning, closely followed by Peter, and after him came a team of trading department personnel from regional office, to do a stock check; an auditor turned up to audit the books, and Joan and various helpers came in to clear up. Besides letting them all in, and out, and seeing to their various needs, Chris dealt with the mail and phone calls, took empty boxes to the shed for burning, moved furniture, reinstated the Red Corridor to normal after its use as an overflow for the shop. . . .

It was December 31st. Tomorrow the whole thing would start again. Next year there would be all the joys of roof re-leading to contend with, going on through March gales which shredded two expensive tarpaulins to tiny pieces and sailed corrugated iron through the air like paper planes; our windows would be floodlit all night for months because of the scaffolding; the roofing work would go on, and on, through into July. . . .

In other words, life at Felbrigg continued, very much as usual.

## Last Word

As I write, we have been at Felbrigg Hall for almost five years and, since Robert's retirement, Chris has been administrator. He doesn't work any less hard, or any fewer hours; we have yet to manage our full holiday entitlement, and as for time off in lieu of bank holidays and so forth . . . well, there's just no point in worrying about things like that.

But there is another, positive side which helps provide a balance. This tree-clad, undulating area of Norfolk is one of the loveliest and most unspoilt in the country. The Hall itself is magnificent, stately and yet homely, and the people we know and meet are a joy. Through Felbrigg our lives have been enriched, not least by the many good friends we have discovered.

It's a pleasure . . . to be part of a close community, among staff and tenants and friends with whom we share a common love for Felbrigg Hall . . . to solve a problem for a visitor in trouble . . . to receive a letter of genuine appreciation . . . to see children realise that history needn't be dry and boring . . . to watch adult faces rapt with interest or amazement . . . to hear someone say how clean the house is now, or what a friendly atmosphere it has . . . and to feel that we can take pride in our own small contribution to all of this.

And, yes, there really are also the occasional touches of almost fairy-tale enchantment. It's magical ... to tread in deep virgin snow marked lightly by the tracks of birds, to see where a fox has walked before us, and on the same day to find the first camellia budding in the orangery ... to spend a golden summer evening on the roof, high above the world, with a glass of wine in one's hand and a pastoral view that stretches for miles with scarcely a house to be seen, all beneath wide skies ablaze with sunset ... to wander through woods rich with autumn, scuffing up crisp leaves, only yards from one's door ... to lean from a window on a clear starry night and listen to carol singers serenading in the courtyard. ...

The life has a little of everything: one day you're playing host to royalty, the next you're up to your elbows in a blocked drain. It's not a job, really, it's a vocation unlike any other and, if you can adjust to it, it offers many compensations in exchange for the huge demands which it undoubtedly makes.

The life has a little of everything

What is there to do in a National Trust mansion? The answer is—whatever each moment brings, dawn to midnight, three hundred and sixty-five days of the year.

This has been mainly the houseman's story. The administrator's story would fill another book.


NB: If you are planning to visit Felbrigg, or any other National Trust property, please check on times and days of opening. *The National Trust Handbook* has all the details, or tourist offices should be able to supply leaflets and information. Enjoy your visit!